Introduction

Mention the word 'watercolour' and what do most people think of? Luminous, glowing works of art in which the paint appears to float as if by magic on the surface of the paper; transparent, wet-into-wet washes that capture the effects of light and shade to perfection; and subtle transitions of colour that are hard – if not impossible – to emulate in any other medium.

Add to this the fact that watercolour paint is relatively inexpensive, easily portable, quick-drying and odour free, and it's hardly surprising that it is by far the most popular painting medium among amateur artists. Indeed, it is estimated that around 80 per cent of all amateurs produce some, if not all, of their work in watercolour.

One of the delights of watercolour is that initially you do not need a lot of materials. In fact a basic palette of 12 to 20 colours, a small handful of brushes, and a pad of watercolour paper are more than enough for most people's needs to begin with. As you practise and develop your own style, you will build up a collection of equipment as you go along.

Once you have bought your basic equipment, the next step is to become thoroughly familiar with the materials that you are using and to learn how they behave. In this book there are more than 25 specially-commissioned full-length projects that cover all the popular subjects – skies and water, portraits and figures, still lifes and animals, landscapes and buildings, and trees and flowers. You will find that each project is easy to follow with detailed colour photographs which illustrate every step.

Do not worry if your first attempts do not look exactly like the ones reproduced here. The most scary thing for every painter is simply getting over initial inhibitions about making marks on a blank sheet of paper, and every brush stroke that you make will teach you something new about how the paint behaves or about your own hand–eye co-ordination. Set aside a little time for painting each day, if you can – and after a couple of

Moroccan kasbah ▼

Here the artist has used complementary colours – the orangey ochres and terracottas of the buildings against the rich blue sky – to create a rich, warm atmosphere.

LEARN TO PAINT WITH
WATERCOLOURS
with 25 step-by-step painting projects

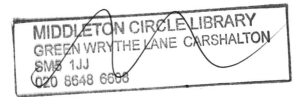

AND IAN SIDAWAY

southwater

This edition is published by Southwater

Southwater is an imprint of Anness Publishing Ltd
Hermes House, 88–89 Blackfriars Road, London SE1 8HA
tel. 020 7401 2077; fax 020 7633 9499
www.southwaterbooks.com; info@anness.com

© Anness Publishing Ltd 2005

UK agent: The Manning Partnership Ltd
6 The Old Dairy, Melcombe Road, Bath BA2 3LR
tel. 01225 478444; fax 01225 478440
sales@manning-partnership.co.uk

UK distributor: Grantham Book Services Ltd
Isaac Newton Way, Alma Park Industrial Estate
Grantham, Lincs NG31 9SD
tel. 01476 541080; fax 01476 541061
orders@gbs.tbs-ltd.co.uk

North American agent/distributor: National Book Network
4501 Forbes Boulevard, Suite 200, Lanham, MD 20706
tel. 301 459 3366; fax 301 429 5746; www.nbnbooks.com

Australian agent/distributor: Pan Macmillan Australia
Level 18, St Martins Tower, 31 Market St, Sydney, NSW 2000
tel. 1300 135 113; fax 1300 135 103;
customer.service@macmillan.com.au

New Zealand agent/distributor: David Bateman Ltd
30 Tarndale Grove, Off Bush Road, Albany, Auckland
tel. (09) 415 7664; fax (09) 415 8892

A CIP catalogue record for this book is available from
the British Library.

Previously published as part of a larger volume,
The Practical Encyclopedia of Watercolour

Publisher: Joanna Lorenz
Editorial Director: Helen Sudell
Senior Editor: Sarah Ainley
Editor: Elizabeth Woodland
Consultant Editor: Sarah Hoggett
Photographers: George Taylor and Nigel Cheffers-Heard
Designer: Nigel Partridge
Cover designer: Nigel Partridge
Illustrator: Ian Sidaway
Project contributors: Ray Balkwill, Diana Constance, Joe Francis
Dowden, Paul Dyson, Abigail Edgar, Wendy Jelbert, Melvyn Petterson,
Paul Robinson, Ian Sidaway, Albany Wiseman
Production Controller: Claire Rae

1 3 5 7 9 10 8 6 4 2

Acknowledgements
The publishers and authors are grateful to Daler-Rowney UK
and Turnham Arts and Crafts for their generous loan of materials
for the photography.
In addition, special thanks must go to the following watercolour
artists for their step-by-step demonstrations:
t = top, b = bottom, l = left, r = right, c = centre.
Ray Balkwill: pages 36–41; Diana Constance: pages 120–125;
Joe Francis Dowden: pages 18–23; 30–35; Paul Dyson: pages 92–93;
100–105; 106–111; Abigail Edgar: pages 44–47; 72–77; 146–151;
152–157; Wendy Jelbert: pages 24–29; 48–51; 58–59; 62–67;
80–85;126–131; Melvyn Petterson: pages 12–15; 94–99;
Paul Robinson: pages 114–119; Ian Sidaway: pages 86–91; 140–145;
Albany Wiseman: pages 8–11; 52–55; 68–69; 134–139.

Copyright paintings and photographs are reproduced in this book
by kind permission of the following:
t = top, b = bottom, l = left, r = right, c = centre.
Trudy Friend: pages 7 (b); 43 (b); Jonathon Hibberd: page 52(t);
Wendy Jelbert: pages 7 (t); 16; 17 (b); 43 (t); 56;
Ian Sidaway: pages 6; 17 (t); 42; 149; George Taylor: 8 (t).

Contents

weeks, look back and assess your progress. You will be amazed at how far you have come.

The subject matter is limitless, from a simple but dramatic study of clouds at sunset to a detailed painting of fishing boats moored in a harbour, from a single sunflower on a white background to a portrait of a much-loved family pet, you will find something here to suit all tastes.

Practise these projects over the course of an afternoon – or you may even decide to spread them out over several painting sessions. You can either copy the projects step by step, exactly as shown here, or use them as a starting point for your own artistic explorations. All the projects are packed with useful tips and general principles that you can apply to subjects of your own choosing – so take the time to study them carefully, even if you do not reproduce them all.

You will find many different approaches here – some finely detailed, with delicate brushwork and careful build-ups of washes; others much looser and more impressionistic. All approaches are valid and you will almost certainly have your own preferences. The most important thing is to realize just how much you can learn from looking at other artists' work. There are special features on a wide range of popular subjects, such as painting skies and water, and painting people, animals and still life. These lively and inspirational works by contemporary artists will provide you with a constant source of inspiration and practical information on how to approach these subjects.

All the artists featured in this book have built up a wealth of experience over many years of study, which they share here with you in the hope that you will gain as much pleasure and enjoyment from painting in watercolour as they have experienced. With time and practice, you will be creating works of art that you can be proud to display.

Summer flower garden ▲
Softly coloured poppies, irises, daisies and delphiniums line a winding path, which leads to the rose-clad arch. The intrigue is in wondering what lies beyond.

Seated figure in interior ▶
When painting someone in a setting, it is important that the focus of the painting must remain the person. This scene is beautifully balanced by a wonderful sense of light and shade.

6

Painting Skies

Skies have always both fascinated and frustrated artists. The fascination comes from the infinite combinations of cloud formations and colours, which can change minute by minute depending on the weather conditions and the time of day, and the frustration from trying to decide on the most appropriate way in which to represent them.

Although skies can be painted as a subject in themselves, they are more commonly viewed as part of a landscape – and an important part, at that. It is from the sky that light comes to illuminate the landscape below, and the colour and mood of all landscapes are directly influenced by the sky above.

When you are painting a sky as part of a landscape, you must make sure that each looks connected and related to the other. The best way to achieve this is to make the sky an integral and important part of the overall composition. As with all things, however, you can exercise a degree of artistic licence. A dramatic and powerful sky can very easily overpower a less interesting landscape, so don't be afraid to alter the balance from what you can actually see in reality.

Although the use of colour is important, particularly when you are painting sunsets, the most critical elements in any sky scene are the cloud formations. Getting to know cloud formations is a useful step towards painting skies well. Artists who paint skies frequently tend to make practice studies of the clouds before they begin.

Beginners often make the mistake of depicting clouds as flat objects against a background of blue, but the reality is very different. Clouds have a top (which the light hits), sides, and a bottom (which is often in deep shadow). They also conform to the laws of perspective, and appear smaller with less distinct colours as they stretch to the horizon. Applying the rules of aerial perspective to clouds can throw up an anomaly, however, for while skies are usually more intense and warmer in colour immediately overhead, becoming cooler and paler nearer the horizon, the exact reverse can be seen on occasions – particularly when looking out to sea, or in large cities with atmospheric pollution.

There are several techniques that you can use to paint clouds successfully. The sky colour and cloud positions might be made using wet-into-wet washes. Cloud shapes can be left as white paper or lifted out using a paper towel or a dry brush. As these washes dry, darker washes can be flooded on to create the parts of the clouds that are in shadow, with more washes being painted over the top to strengthen colour or redefine shapes when the first washes are dry.

Alternatively, you could paint the sky using only wet on dry washes, assessing the colour and tone of each so that the shape and colour of the clouds are built up in layers. Avoid hard edges, which look out of place in a sky scene. Cloud edges can be softened periodically by using clean water and a brush or by blotting with a natural sponge or paper towel.

The Thames at Richmond ▼
In this expansive view, the landscape and the sky are of equal importance. Placing the horizon on the halfway mark is risky, but the image works because the carefully arranged cloud formations balance the intricate landscape. The clouds were created by means of carefully planned wet on dry washes. The blue colour in the sky was painted last, with the cloud shapes being "cut out" as it was applied.

Storm clouds ▲
This loose impression of storm clouds gathering in a pale grey sky uses the same colours as the dark, wet landscape below. Washes were applied wet into wet in order to give a feeling of indistinct focus, which is often apparent in falling rain.

Sunset ▼
A gradated pale blue wash provided the foundation for this sunset. The pale orange strip of light on the horizon takes on an added brilliance seen against the dark landscape and the deep grey clouds above.

Tips: • Use clouds to balance dominant elements in the landscape.
• Take care not to make clear blue skies dominate your landscapes as, without clouds to add interest, such skies tend to look flat and boring.
• Remember that skies and clouds conform to the same laws of perspective as the land. As a general rule, colours get paler the nearer they are to the horizon, with clouds becoming smaller and less distinct.
• Practise painting various wash and cloud combinations. Only by knowing what your materials can do and how they behave will you be free to concentrate on creating the effects you want.

Clouds at sunset

The presence of a few clouds in the sky almost always adds to the drama of a sunset, as the clouds pick up reflected light and add textural interest that might otherwise be lacking.

This project is an excuse to have fun and to play around with wet-into-wet washes to see what effects you can create. Although the wet-into-wet technique is perfect for depicting the gradual transitions of colour that you find in a sunset, it is also notoriously unpredictable. Different papers give different effects, and the degree of wetness also plays an important part. Knowing how wet the paper should be to create a particular effect is something that comes with practice, so don't despair if things initially turn out very differently from what you'd expected. Instead of aiming for a photo-realistic rendition, with every cloud and subtle tonal change in exactly the "right" place, use the scene as a starting point for your explorations: let the flowing paint do the work and adapt your ideas as you go, responding to the shapes and colours that emerge.

Include a hint of the land beneath in a sunset painting, even if it's just a tiny sliver at the very base of the picture. This anchors the image and provides a context for the visual feast above.

Materials
- *140lb (300gsm) rough watercolour paper, pre-stretched*
- *Watercolour paints: cobalt blue, cerulean blue, cadmium yellow, cadmium red, alizarin crimson, ultramarine violet*
- *Brushes: large round*
- *Sponge*

The original scene
Pinks, oranges and violets; glowering clouds fringed with a pure and intense light: a sunset guaranteed to take away the breath of even the most hardened cynic! Clouds like these, with dramatic contrasts of light and dark, are generally much more interesting than fluffy white clouds in a brilliant blue sky.

Reflected light on these clouds provides a much-needed "lift" of colour.

These brooding clouds dominate the scene and add textural interest.

1 Using a large round brush, dampen the paper with clean water, leaving a few areas untouched. Mix a deep blue from cobalt blue and a little cerulean blue and lay a gradated wash, fading to almost nothing and stopping about halfway down the paper.

2 Mix a pale orange from cadmium yellow and a little cadmium red. Using a large round brush, wash this mixture over the lower half of the painting and dot it into the sky, where the setting sun catches the top of some of the cloud formations.

3 Touch the orange mixture into the dry cloud shapes left in Step 1. Working quickly, while the paper is still damp, deepen the orange colour on the lower half of the painting. Mix a dark purple from cobalt blue, alizarin crimson and ultramarine violet and drop this mixture into the centre of the painting, so that the colours blur.

4 Add more purple across the middle of the painting, going into both the blue and the orange areas, to establish the dark bank of cloud that runs across the centre of the image. Leave to dry completely before moving on to the next stage.

5 Dip a sponge in water, squeeze out any excess water and stroke it across the top half of the paper.

6 Using a large round brush, touch the purple mixture used in Step 3 into the dark clouds at the top.

7 Using the same paint mixtures as before, continue touching colour into damp areas, allowing it to spread and find its own way. Watch what happens rather than starting out with preconceived ideas: you will find that the paint suggests shapes that you can then strengthen and make an integral part of the painting.

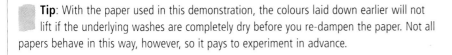

Tip: With the paper used in this demonstration, the colours laid down earlier will not lift if the underlying washes are completely dry before you re-dampen the paper. Not all papers behave in this way, however, so it pays to experiment in advance.

▶

Clouds at sunset

This is an expressive painting, with subtle shifts from one colour to another, which demonstrates one of the main attributes of watercolour – its translucency – to the full. Although it is not a painstaking copy of the original scene, it nonetheless captures the quality of the light and the sense of rapidly changing lighting conditions very well.

The artist has exploited the unpredictability of the wet-into-wet technique by responding to changes as they occur on the paper, and so the painting has a lovely sense of freshness and spontaneity. At the same time he has paid careful attention to the light and dark areas so that the clouds really do look three-dimensional.

Successive wet-into-wet applications build up depth of tone.

Silhouetted shapes on the horizon anchor the scene.

The rough surface of the paper also helps to add textural interest.

Variation: **Clouds at sunset painted on smooth paper**

The same scene painted on smooth paper gives a rather different result. In the previous painting, the rough texture of the paper played an important role. In this painting, however, the smooth surface means that there is a more uniform band of colour across the top of the image. The paint also behaves differently on smooth paper: although this scene was also painted by dropping colour wet into wet, there are a number of hard-edged rings. It is impossible to say that one type of surface is better than the other for this type of work: it is entirely down to personal preference.

Allowing some of the initial wash to show through is an effective technique for skies.

On smooth paper, hard-edged rings of colour sometimes appear.

The paint goes on smoothly, and the paper texture is less evident.

Storm clouds and rainbow

Watercolour is a wonderful medium for painting clouds. The translucency of the paint enables you to create a feeling of light and air, while wet-into-wet washes are perfect for creating subtle transitions from one colour to another.

One of the most important things to remember is that you need to make your clouds look like solid, three-dimensional forms, not just wispy trails of vapour in the sky. Clouds have a top, a bottom and a side. The top usually faces the sun and is therefore lighter than the side and the bottom. Before you start painting, work out which direction the light is coming from so that you can decide which areas of cloud are in shadow and need to be darker in tone.

Make sure that any changes in tone are very gradual. You can soften colours where necessary by lifting off paint with a piece of kitchen paper or a sponge, but try to avoid hard edges at all costs.

The rules of perspective that apply to painting land also apply to painting the sky, and clouds that are further away will appear smaller than those that are immediately overhead. They will also be lighter in tone.

In this project, dramatic banks of cumulus cloud before an evening storm are the focus of interest and the land below is almost an irrelevance. Although the land is so dark that relatively little detail is visible, it is an important part of the picture, as it provides a context for the scene and an anchor for the painting as a whole. In any landscape, the sky must relate to the land beneath and so you need to continually assess the tonal balance between the two.

Materials
- *2B pencil*
- *140lb (300gsm) rough watercolour paper*
- *Watercolour paints: yellow ochre, cadmium lemon, sap green, raw umber, ultramarine blue, cadmium yellow, Prussian blue, cadmium red, burnt sienna, alizarin crimson, viridian*
- *Brushes: medium round, fine round, large wash*
- *Kitchen paper*

The original scene
This is a dramatic and unusual sky. Although the clouds and rainbow provide the main focus of interest, the low-angled early evening sunlight picks out enough detail on the land to relieve the monotony of the dark foreground.

Silhouetted tree shapes provide a visual link between sky and ground.

Low-angled sunlight picks out the house and a patch of the foreground field.

1 Using a 2B pencil, outline the tree shapes on the horizon. Mix a very pale wash of yellow ochre and, using a medium round brush, loosely brush it over the sky, leaving gaps for the lightest areas. Mix cadmium lemon and sap green and brush the mixture over the lightest areas of the fields. Mix a dilute wash of dark brown from raw umber and a touch of ultramarine blue and brush it on to the clouds in the top left of the picture. Add more ultramarine blue to the brown mixture and brush loose strokes over the base of the clouds on the right.

2 While the sky is still damp, add more raw umber to the mixture and brush short calligraphic strokes over the clouds to delineate the lower edges, dabbing some of the paint off with kitchen paper to soften the edges. Mix a dark olive green from cadmium yellow and ultramarine blue and block in the dark areas of the foreground and the silhouetted shapes on the horizon.

3 While the foreground is still damp, mix a bluish green from cadmium yellow, ultramarine blue and Prussian blue and brush it over the foreground to darken it. Mix a warm yellowish green from cadmium lemon and cadmium red with a little ultramarine and brush the mixture over the brightest areas of the fields, which are illuminated by shafts of low-angled evening sunlight.

4 Finish blocking in the silhouettes on the skyline. Mix an orangey red from cadmium red and yellow ochre and, using a medium round brush, block in the shape of the distant house.

Tip: The only details you need on the house are the roof and walls. The rules of perspective make further detail, such as windows, unnecessary.

Assessment time
With the addition of a hint of blue sky and the dark hedge that marks the boundary between the house and the field, the painting is really starting to take shape. The foreground is very dark, and so the next stage is to work on the sky so that the picture has a better overall balance.

The sky is too pale to hold any interest.

The foreground is oppressively dark; the sky needs to be much stronger to balance it.

Note how the red house immediately attracts the eye, even though it occupies only a small area.

5 Mix a rich, dark brown from ultramarine blue and burnt sienna. Using a large wash brush, loosely scrub it into the left-hand side of the sky, leaving a gap for the rainbow and dabbing off paint with kitchen paper to soften the edges. Note how this creates interesting streaks in the sky.

6 Using the same colour, make a series of short calligraphic strokes on the sky at the base of the clouds. The clouds are lit from above, so giving them dark bases helps to establish a sense of form. Brush yellow ochre on to the sky above the dark clouds.

7 Again, dab off paint with kitchen paper to get rid of any obvious brushstrokes and create interesting streaks and wispy textures in the clouds. The clouds should look as if they are swirling overhead, their brooding presence dominating the entire scene.

8 Using a darker version of the mixture, darken the clouds again so that the sky has more impact. You need to continually assess the tones in a painting like this, as an alteration to one area can disrupt the tonal balance of the painting as a whole.

9 Finally, paint the rainbow, using a very fine round brush and long, confident strokes. There is no distinct demarcation between one colour and the next, so it doesn't matter if the colours merge. If you do want to boost any of the colours, allow the paint to dry and then strengthen the colours with a second application.

Storm clouds and rainbow

This is a bold and dramatic interpretation of glowering storm clouds. In the sky, the paint is applied in thin, transparent layers, softened in places by dabbing off paint with kitchen paper, and the white of the paper is allowed to show through, creating a wonderful feeling of luminosity. The land below, in contrast, is solid and dark and forms a complete counterpoint to the rapidly moving clouds above.

Successive layers of colour applied quite thickly in the foreground create a feeling of solidity.

The clouds have an airy texture, achieved by applying the paint wet into wet and then dabbing it off with kitchen paper.

A shaft of warm, evening sunlight leads the viewer's eye across the painting.

Painting Water

Watercolour is, by its very nature, the perfect material for painting water. Its fluidity and transparency, and its habit of puddling, pooling and generally behaving in an unpredictable way, are characteristics that can be used to great effect.

The colour and appearance of water are heavily influenced by the predominant weather conditions, the reflected colours and shapes in the environment, and the colours of any rocks, sand or vegetation seen beneath the surface. The sea is blue because it reflects the sky, for example, while a pond deep in the woods looks deep and foreboding because it reflects the dark foliage of the surrounding trees.

Several watercolour techniques are particularly suited to painting water. Broad wash techniques, using as large a brush as possible, should be used to paint large expanses of water. Washes can be worked wet on wet to suggest subtle colour changes, or wet on dry to suggest wave or ripple shapes or reflected objects and colours.

Broken colour techniques using a dry brush dragged across rough paper give the impression of ripples or dappled sunlight. Scraping back into wet paint, using a cut-off piece of card or one of the purpose-made rubber paint shapers, is a particularly good way of representing ripples, especially on smooth, hot-pressed paper. Highlights in the water can be created by scratching back to reveal white paper or by applying masking fluid prior to making any washes.

> **Tips:** • Always follow the rules of perspective. Waves of equal size will appear smaller the further away from you they are, while colour becomes less intense and cooler and detail is less evident.
> • Note how objects in the water are slightly distorted due to the way light waves are refracted. The colours of objects reflected in water are generally less intense and more subdued than the colours of the objects themselves.

Talbert

◄ Waterfall
White body colour was applied using a mixture of fluid wash and drybrush techniques to capture the light catching on the falling water as it tumbles over rocks and boulders. The stones and boulders were painted using a texture paste to give them added form.

8 a.m, Venice Lagoon ▲

This painting, made as the early-morning light highlighted the ripples on the water, uses carefully applied wet-on-dry washes. The dappled sunlight on the water surface was created by applying masking fluid prior to making any washes. Colours were kept crisp and clean by using no more than three overlapping washes. Note how the ripples conform to the laws of perspective by getting smaller as they get closer to the horizon.

◄ Willows

Wet-into-wet washes lay the foundation and general shape of the reflections of these riverside trees. Wet-on-dry washes define the shapes further, while a little linear brush and coloured pencil work hint at a slight breeze rippling the almost still surface.

> **Tip**: Choose a surface to complement the subject. A rough sea will look rougher if painted on a rough-surface paper, while a smooth, hot-pressed paper is ideal for a painting of a tranquil, mirror-like pond.

Woodland waterfall

Waterfalls offer particular challenges to watercolour artists. Not only do you have to paint a liquid that lacks any real colour of its own but takes its colour from its surroundings, but you also need to make that liquid look wet and convey a sense of how quickly it is moving.

As always, the key is to try to convey an overall impression, rather than get caught up in attempting to recreate life, and paint every single water droplet and leaf. Before you start painting, and even before you make your first preliminary sketch, stop and think about what it is that appeals to you in the scene. Is it the intensity of the rushing water or the sunlight sparkling on the water surface? Is the waterfall itself the most important feature or are the surroundings just as interesting? This will help you to decide on the main focus of interest in your painting – and armed with this knowledge, you can decide how best to tackle the painting as a whole.

In real life, all your senses come into play: you can hear the water cascading down and feel the dappled sunlight on your face. In a painting, however, you have to convey these qualities through visual means alone. Sometimes this means you need to exaggerate certain aspects in order to get the message across – making the spray more dramatic, perhaps, or altering the composition to remove distracting features or make interesting ones more prominent.

Materials
- *B pencil*
- *Tracing paper*
- *140lb (300gsm) NOT watercolour paper, pre-stretched*
- *Watercolour paints: cadmium lemon, phthalocyanine green, Payne's grey, burnt sienna, phthalocyanine blue, alizarin crimson*
- *Brushes: large round, fine round, medium wash, old brush for masking fluid*
- *Masking fluid*
- *Low-tack masking tape*
- *Drawing paper to make mask*
- *Household candle*
- *Gum arabic*

The original scene
Although the scene is attractive, the lighting is flat and the colours dull. Here, the artist decided he needed to increase the contrast between light and shade. To do this, you need to carefully work out which areas will be hit by light from above and which will be in shadow. He also increased the size of the pool below the waterfall: paradoxically, the waterfall itself has more impact if it is surrounded by calmer areas.

The waterfall ends too near the bottom of the frame.

The colours are very subdued. Increasing the contrast between light and shade will make the painting more interesting.

1 Using a B pencil, make a sketch on tracing paper to establish the main lines of your subject and work out the size and shape of your painting. When you are happy with the result, transfer your tracing on to pre-stretched watercolour paper.

2 Place a sheet of white drawing paper between the watercolour paper and the tracing paper and draw around the waterfall area. Cut out the shape of the waterfall and place it in position on the watercolour paper as a mask, fixing it in place with low-tack masking tape. Gently rub a household candle over the area of water below the waterfall, keeping the strokes very loose. This will preserve some of the white of the paper and add an interesting texture.

3 Using an old brush, apply masking fluid over the white lines of the waterfall. Leave to dry.

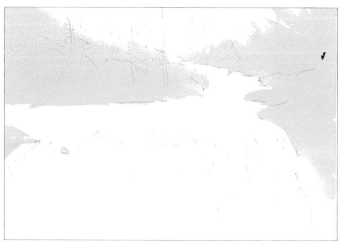

4 Apply masking fluid to the bright highlight area of sky at the top of the picture area and leave to dry. Using a large round brush, brush clean water over the trees. Mix a strong wash of cadmium lemon and brush it over all the damp areas. Leave to dry.

5 Mask off the water area with paper. Mix a mid-toned green from cadmium lemon and a little phthalocyanine green. Holding a fine round brush at the same angle at which the branches grow, spatter water across the top of the picture. Spatter the damp area with green paint. Leave to dry.

6 Continue spattering first with water and then with the green mixture of phthalocyanine green and cadmium lemon, as in Step 5, until you achieve the right density of tone in the trees. Leave each application of spattering to dry completely before you apply the next one.

Tip: Spattering clean water on to the paper first, before you spatter on the paint mixture, means that the paint will spread and blur on the wet paper. If you spatter the paint on to dry paper, you will create crisply defined blobs of colour – a very different effect.

▶

7 Add Payne's grey to the phthalocyanine green and cadmium lemon mixture and, using a fine brush, put in the very dark tones along the water's edge in order to define the edge of the river bank.

8 Using a fine brush, brush burnt sienna between the leaves adjoining the dark spattered areas. Mix a rich brown from burnt sienna and Payne's grey and paint the tree trunks and branches. Leave to dry.

9 Using your fingertips, gently rub and peel the masking fluid off the sky area. The sky area is very bright in comparison with the rest of the scene, and so it is important to reserve these light areas in the early part of the painting – even though they will be toned down very slightly in the later stages.

Assessment time

The surrounding woodland is now almost complete. Before you go any further, make sure you've put in as much detail as you want here. The water takes its colour from what's reflected in it. Because of this it is essential that you establish the scenery around the waterfall before you begin to put in any of the water detail.

The line of the riverbank is crisply painted, establishing the course of the river.

The rocks in the waterfall have been marked in pencil, providing an underlying structure for the scene.

10 Using masking fluid, mask the long strokes of white that cascade down from the waterfall into the pool below. Leave to dry. Using a medium wash brush, brush clean water horizontally across the top of the water above the waterfall. Brush a little gum arabic on to the damp area. Keeping the brush fairly dry in order to control the colour, brush vertical strokes of phthalocyanine blue mixed with a little alizarin crimson and burnt sienna on to the damp area.

11 Brush straight lines of Payne's grey across the top of the waterfall to denote the edge over which the water topples. Mix Payne's grey with phthalocyanine blue and brush on to the waterfall itself, using a drybrush technique. On the lower part of the fall, make the marks longer and rougher to indicate the increased speed of the water. Leave to dry.

12 Re-wet the pool above the fall. Using a fine, round brush, touch cadmium lemon into the damp area. Dab on vertical strokes of cadmium lemon, burnt sienna, and phthalocyanine green for the tree trunk reflections. The colours will merge together and the fact that they are blurred helps to convey the wetness of the water.

13 Brush burnt sienna mixed with Payne's grey on to the cascade of water than runs into the pool.

Tip: By applying clean water to the surface before you paint, the strokes diffuse and blur, giving soft blends rather than hard-edged streaks of colour.

14 Working from the bottom of the waterfall upwards, brush a mixture of Payne's grey and phthalocyanine blue into the waterfall. Note how the texture of the candle wax shows through. Keep the brush quite dry, dabbing off excess paint on kitchen paper, if necessary. Add a little alizarin crimson to the mixture for the darker water at the base of the fall.

15 Paint the rocks under the waterfall in a mixture of Payne's grey, phthalocyanine blue and a little alizarin crimson. Use the same mixture to paint more rocks poking up through the foam of the water. Drybrush water along the left and right edges of the painting and apply the rock colour – again with an almost dry brush. The paint will spread down into the damp area.

16 Stipple little dots of masking fluid on to the base of the pool below the waterfall for the white bubbles of foam. Leave to dry. Apply a light wash of phthalocyanine blue mixed with a little Payne's grey over the pool below the waterfall, brushing the paint on with loose, horizontal strokes. While the paint is still damp, run in a few darker vertical lines of the same mixture. Leave to dry.

17 Using a large brush and a darker version of the phthalocyanine blue and Payne's grey mixture, paint the dark area at the base of the pool with bold, zigzag-shaped brushstrokes. Leave to dry.

18 Using your fingertips, gently rub off the masking fluid on the lower half of the painting. Stand back and assess the tonal values of the painting as a whole. If the exposed area looks too white and stark, you may need to touch in some colour in the water areas to redress the overall balance of the scene.

Woodland waterfall

This is a very lively rendition of a waterfall in full spate, which conveys the mood and atmosphere of the scene rather than capturing every leaf and twig in painstaking detail. Much of the paper is left white, in order to convey the full force of the rushing water. The painting has a stronger feeling of light and shade than the original photo, and hence more impact.

The white of the paper conveys the cascading, foaming water.

Skilful use of the wet-into-wet technique has allowed colours to merge on the paper, creating realistic-looking reflections.

Longer brushstrokes in the lower part of the waterfall help to create an impression of movement in the water.

Crashing waves

This project depicts a massive sea wave just as it is about to break over craggy rocks. Your challenge is to capture the energy and power of the scene.

Few people would go as far in their search for realism as the great landscape artist J.M.W. Turner, who is reputed to have tied himself to a ship's mast in order to experience the full force of a storm at sea. Fortunately, there are easier and less perilous ways of adding drama to your seascapes.

The first thing to think about is your viewpoint. Construct your painting as if you are viewing the scene from a low viewpoint, so that the waves seem to tower above you.

For maximum drama, capture the waves while they are building or when they are at their peak, just before they break and come crashing down. You can gauge the height of the waves by comparing them with nearby rocks or clifftops, while including such features in your painting will provide you with both a focal point and a sense of scale.

Try to attune yourself to the sea's natural rhythms. Watch the ebb and flow of the waves and concentrate on holding the memory of this rhythm in your mind as you are painting. This will help you to capture the energy of the scene.

Finally, remember that water takes its colour from objects in and around it. You may be surprised at how many different colours there are in a scene like this.

Materials
- *4B pencil*
- *140lb (300gsm) NOT watercolour paper, pre-stretched*
- *Watercolour paints: Payne's grey, phthalocyanine blue, cadmium yellow, lemon yellow, Hooker's green, cerulean blue, yellow ochre, raw sienna, sepia, violet, burnt sienna, cobalt blue*
- *Gouache paints: permanent white*
- *Brushes: medium round, fine round*
- *Mixing or palette knife*
- *Fine texture paste*
- *Ruling drawing pen*
- *Masking fluid*
- *Sponge*

The original scene
It is notoriously difficult to photograph a breaking wave at exactly the right moment, and so the artist used this photograph merely to remind herself of the energy of the scene and the shapes and colours.

Reference sketches
Tonal sketches are a very good way of working out the light and dark areas of the scene. You will find that it helps to think of the waves as solid, three-dimensional objects, with a light and a shaded side. Try several versions so that you get used to the way the waves break over the rocks.

1 Using a 4B pencil, lightly sketch the scene, putting in the foreground rocks and the main waves. Take time to get the angles of the waves right: it is vital that they look as if they are travelling at speed and are just about to come crashing down.

2 Using a palette knife, apply fine texture paste over the rocks. Leave to dry. (Texture paste is available in several grades; the coarser it is, the more pronounced the effect. Here, the wave is more important than the rocks, so fine texture paste is sufficient).

3 Using a ruling drawing pen, apply masking fluid over the crest of the main wave and dot in flecks and swirls of foam in the water. Using a small sponge, dab masking fluid on to selected areas of the sea to create softer foamy areas. Leave to dry.

4 Mix a mid-toned wash of Payne's grey and another of phthalocyanine blue. Dampen the sky area with clean water and brush Payne's grey on to the right-hand side and phthalocyanine blue on to the left-hand side. Leave to dry.

5 Mix a strong wash of cadmium yellow with a touch of lemon yellow. Dampen the waves with clean water and lightly brush the bright yellow paint mixture over the tops of the waves.

▶

6 While the first wash is still wet, brush Hooker's green into the yellow so that the colours merge together. Mix a darker green from Hooker's green, phthalocyanine blue and a little cadmium yellow and brush this mixture into the lower part of the waves, feathering the mixture up into the yellow so that the colours blend imperceptibly on the paper. Brush over this darker green several times to build up the necessary density of tone.

7 Mix a dark blue from phthalocyanine blue and cerulean blue and brush this mixture into the lower part of the large wave, feathering the colour upwards. Because the previous washes are still wet the colours spread and merge together on the paper, building up darker tones without completely blocking out the underlying colours. Use loose, swift brushstrokes and try to capture the energy and power of the sea.

8 Mix a mid-toned wash of yellow ochre and brush it over the texture paste on the rocks, adding raw sienna and sepia for the dark foreground.

Tip: Allow the colour to "drift" into the sea so that it looks as if the sea is washing over the rocks. Unless you do this the rocks will simply look as if they are floating on the water.

9 Mix a greyish blue from violet and Hooker's green. Brush little touches of this colour into the waves and into the pools at the base of the rocks, making swirling brushstrokes to help convey the movement of the water.

10 Using the dark green mixture from Step 6 and the brown used on the rocks, put a few dark accents into the waves. Soften the brushstrokes by brushing them with clean water to blend them into the other wave colours.

11 When you are sure that the paint is completely dry, gently rub off the masking fluid with your fingertips to reveal the foaming crests of the waves and the spattered highlights on the water.

Assessment time

Now that all the masking fluid has been removed, you can see how effectively the white of the paper has been reserved for the swirls and flecks of foam in the sea. However, these areas now look glaringly white and stark: they need to be toned down so that they become an integral part of the scene. However, you will need to take great care not to lose the very free, spontaneous nature of the swirling lines or the water will start to look too static and overworked. The contrast between the light and the very dark areas also needs to be strengthened a little in order to give a better feeling of the volume of the waves.

The exposed areas are much too bright.

The colours work well in this area, but there is not enough of a sense of the direction in which the water is moving.

12 Mix an opaque mauve from permanent white gouache, violet and a tiny touch of burnt sienna. Brush this mixture under the crest of the main wave, so that it looks like shadows under the very bright, white foam.

13 The exposed white areas look too stark against the dark colours of the water and rocks. Mix a very pale opaque blue from cobalt blue and permanent white gouache and cover up the exposed swirls of white in the water.

14 Soften the harsh markings by brushing over more of the cobalt blue and gouache mixture. Paint some swirls of white gouache at the base of the main wave. Putting a little opaque colour into the water helps to give it some solidity.

15 Spatter a few specks of white gouache above the crest of the wave for the flecks of foam that fly into the air. Don't overdo it: too much gouache could easily overpower the light, translucent watercolour washes that you've worked so hard to create.

16 Spatter a few specks of the cobalt blue and white gouache mixture above the rocks. (This area is very dark and pure white gouache would look too stark.)

17 Stand back from the painting and assess the tonal values. You may find that you need to darken some of the colours in the centre of the painting.

18 Using the same dark brown mixture as before, build up the tones on the rocks. They need to stand out from the water that surrounds them.

Crashing waves

This is a dramatic and carefully observed painting that captures the energy of the scene to perfection. Note the many different tones in the water and the way the brushstrokes echo the motion of the waves. The rocks provide solidity and a sense of scale, but do not detract from the large wave that is hurtling forwards.

Spattering is the perfect technique for depicting foam-flecked waves.

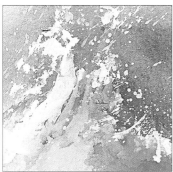

Dark tones in this area contrast with the light edge of the breaking wave and help to give it volume.

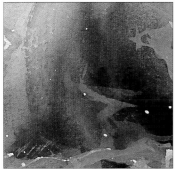

The rocks provide a necessary point of solidity in the scene.

Loose, swirling brushstrokes capture the motion of the sea.

Lake with reflections

Who could resist the bright, sunny colours of this lakeside scene in the heat of the summer, with its reflections of hillsides covered in trees? Any artist would be happy to while away a few hours sketching and painting in such a tranquil setting.

However, straightforward symmetrical reflections can sometimes look a little boring and predictable, so look out for other things that will add interest to your paintings. Sweeping curves, such as the foreshore on the right in this scene, help to lead the viewer's eye through the picture, while interesting textures are always a bonus.

This project also provides you with the challenge of painting partially submerged objects. Here you need to think about the rules of perspective: remember that things look paler and smaller the further away they are. As an added complication, the way that water refracts lights also distorts the shape of submerged objects. Trust your eyes and paint what you see, rather than assuming you know what shape things actually are.

Materials
- *B pencil*
- *Tracing paper*
- *140lb (300gsm) NOT watercolour paper, pre-stretched*
- *Watercolour paints: alizarin crimson, Naples yellow, phthalocyanine blue, phthalocyanine green, burnt sienna, French ultramarine, Payne's grey, quinacridone magenta*
- *Brushes: medium round, fine round, old brush for masking fluid*
- *Masking fluid*
- *Gum arabic*
- *Kitchen paper*

> **Tip**: Leave the tracing paper attached to one side of the watercolour paper, so that you can flip it back over if necessary during the painting process and reaffirm any lines and shapes that have been covered by paint.

The original scene
You can almost feel the heat of the sun when you look at this photograph of a lake in southern Spain. The foreshore and hillside are dry and dusty, while the lake itself appears to be slowly evaporating, exposing rocks in the shallows. Because of the angle at which the photograph was taken, the colours are actually less intense than they were in real life. The artist decided to exaggerate the colours slightly to emphasize the feeling of heat.

The distant mountains are muted in colour and will benefit from being made more intense in the painting.

Much of the foreground is made up of submerged stones. You could put some exposed stones in this area to add interest.

1 Using a B pencil, make an initial sketch on tracing paper to establish the main lines of your subject. When you are happy with the result, trace your sketch on to pre-stretched watercolour paper. Using an old brush, apply masking fluid to some of the large foreground stones. Leave to dry.

2 Mix alizarin crimson with a little Naples yellow and, using a medium round brush, brush the mixture over the mountains and up into the sky. Leave to dry. Mix a bright blue from phthalocyanine blue and a little phthalocyanine green. Dampen the sky with clear water and, while the paper is still wet, brush on the blue mixture, stopping along the ridge and drawing the colour down into the mountains. Leave to dry.

3 Mix a mid-toned orangey brown from Naples yellow and burnt sienna, and paint the dry and dusty foreshore of the lake, dropping in more burnt sienna for the darker areas. Leave to dry.

4 Mix a purplish grey from burnt sienna, French ultramarine and alizarin crimson. Using a fine round brush, brush clean water across the mountains and then brush on marks of the grey mixture. Leave to dry.

5 Make up more of the burnt sienna and Naples yellow mixture and, using a medium round brush, paint the arid, sandy background on the top right of the painting. While this area is still wet, mix an olive green from phthalocyanine green, burnt sienna and a little Naples yellow and, using a medium round brush, paint in the loose shapes of trees and bushes. Paint the shadow areas in the trees in the same purplish grey mix used in Step 4. Leave to dry.

▶

6 Paint more trees on the left-hand side of the painting in the same way. Brush clean water across the sky. Mix Payne's grey with a little phthalocyanine green and, using the tip of the brush, dot this mixture into the damp sky area to denote the trees that stand out above the skyline. The colour will blur slightly. Leave to dry.

7 Using a B pencil, map out a few more stones on the shoreline. Mix a warm brown from burnt sienna and French ultramarine and brush in on to the foreground, working around the stones. Add more French ultramarine to the mixture and paint shadows around the edges of the stones to establish a three-dimensional effect. Leave to dry.

8 Brush clean water over the lake area. Mix burnt sienna with a little quinacridone magenta and, using a medium round brush, wash this mixture loosely over the shallow foreground of the lake, where partially submerged stones are clearly visible.

9 While the lake is still damp, brush phthalocyanine blue over the centre of the lake, adding a little quinacridone magenta as you work down over the stones in the foreground. Apply a second layer of the same colours over the same area and leave to dry.

Assessment time

Wet the blank area at the top of the lake and brush gum arabic on to the damp area. Using a fine brush, brush on vertical strokes of Naples yellow, burnt sienna, quinacridone magenta mixed with French ultramarine, and the olive green mixture used in Step 5. Leave to dry.

With the reflections in place, the painting is nearing its final stages. All that remains to be done is to put in some of the fine detail. Step back and think carefully about how you are going to do this. Far from making the painting look more realistic, too much detail would actually detract from the fresh, spontaneous quality of the overall scene.

This area lacks visual interest. Adding submerged stones here will indicate both the clarity of the water and how shallow it is at this point.

These stones look as if they're floating on the surface of the water.

10 Dip a medium round brush in clean water and gently lift off the flattened, elongated shapes of underwater stones, varying the sizes. You may need to stroke the brush backwards and forwards several times on the paper in order to loosen the paint.

11 As you lift off each shape, dab the area firmly with clean kitchen paper to remove any excess water. Turn and re-fold the kitchen paper each time you use it, to prevent the risk of dabbing paint back on.

▶

12 The submerged stones in the foreground of the lake add visual interest to what would otherwise be a dull, blank area of the scene, but as yet they do not look three-dimensional. The large stones above the surface of the water and on the shoreline also need more texture if they are to look convincing.

13 Mix a dark brown shadow colour from burnt sienna and French ultramarine and, using a medium round brush, use this mixture to loosely paint the shadows underneath the submerged stones. This makes the stones look three-dimensional and allows them to stand out more clearly from the base of the lake. It also adds texture to the base of the lake. Leave to dry.

14 Using a fine brush, wet the area at the base of the reflection and touch in a mixture of French ultramarine and alizarin crimson to soften the edges. Mix burnt sienna with a little French ultramarine and use it to touch in the shadows under the largest rocks on the shoreline. Leave to dry. Using your fingertips, gently rub off the masking fluid.

15 Using a fine, almost dry brush, brush water over the exposed rocks and then drop in a very pale wash of burnt sienna. Leave to dry. Drybrush a darker mixture of burnt sienna on to the rocks in places, for dark accents. To make the rocks look more three-dimensional, stroke on a little French ultramarine for the shadow areas.

Lake with reflections

This is a truly inviting image. The lake looks so realistic that you want to dabble your toes in it, while the feeling of heat is almost tangible.

The artist's skilful use of complementary colours (the bright blue of the sky set against the rich orangey brown of the stones and earth) has helped to create a really vibrant painting.

Textural details, such as the dry brushwork on the rocks and the distant trees painted wet into wet, are subtle but effective, while the careful blending of colours in the reflections conveys the stillness of the water perfectly. The composition is simple, but the foreshore leads the eye in a sweeping curve right through the painting.

The lake is not a uniform blue throughout, but takes its colour from the objects that are reflected in it, as well as from the visible shallow areas.

A judiciously placed shadow under one edge of the stones helps to make them look three-dimensional.

The easiest way to paint the reflection of the small rocks in the distance is simply to paint a thin line of burnt sienna right through the middle.

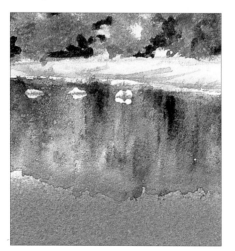

Harbour moorings

Ports and harbours are a never-ending source of inspiration for artists. The scene is constantly moving as the tide ebbs and flows, and the changing seasons bring different weather and lighting conditions. Reflections in the water, patterns in the sand, and countless details from boat masts to barnacles: there are thousands of things to stir the imagination. It's not just a visual feast: the sound of lapping water and squawking gulls, and the smell of seaweed combine to make this one of the most satisfying of all subjects to paint.

The key is to plan ahead and think about what you want to convey. Harbours are busy places, with lots of things going on and a host of fascinating details and textures to distract the eye, and you will almost invariably need to simplify things when you're painting. Decide on your main focus of interest and construct your painting around it. You may find that you need to alter the position of certain elements within the picture space, or to subdue some details that draw attention away from the main subject and place more emphasis on others.

This particular project uses a wide range of classic watercolour techniques to create a timeless scene of a working harbour at low tide. Pay attention to the reflections and the way the light catches the water: these are what will make the painted scene come to life, and there is no better medium for these transient effects of the light than watercolour.

Materials
- *4B graphite pencil*
- *140lb (300gsm) NOT watercolour paper, pre-stretched*
- *Watercolour paints: cadmium orange, Naples yellow, phthalocyanine blue, cerulean blue, permanent rose, raw sienna, ultramarine blue, burnt umber, cadmium red, burnt sienna, light red*
- *Gouache paints: permanent white*
- *Brushes: old brush for masking, 1in (2.5cm) hake, small round, medium filbert, fine filbert, fine rigger*
- *Masking fluid*
- *Masking tape*
- *Plastic ruler or straightedge*

The original scene
The tilted boats, wet sand and textures on the harbour wall all have the potential to make an interesting painting, but the sky and water are a little bland and there is no real focus of interest.

The town on the far side of the estuary is a little distracting.

The boats form a straight line across the image; it is unclear where the main focus of interest lies.

Preliminary sketch
The artist decided to make more of the water in his painting, introducing reflections that were not there in real life. He made this preliminary charcoal sketch to work out the tonal values of the scene. He then decided that the boats were too close together and that the scene was too cramped. In his final version, therefore, he widened the image so that the right-hand boat was further away; he also introduced two figures walking across the sand to provide a sense of scale.

1 Using a 4B graphite pencil, sketch the scene, putting in the outlines of the harbour wall, distant hill, boats and figures and indicating the different bands of sand and water in the foreground.

2 Using an old brush, apply masking fluid over the foreground water and the brightly lit right-hand side of the main boat to protect the highlight areas that you want to remain white in the finished painting. To get fine, straight lines, place a plastic ruler or straightedge on its side, rest the ferrule of the brush on top and gently glide the brush along.

3 Spatter a little masking fluid over the foreground of the scene to suggest some random texture and highlights in the sand and water. Be careful not to overdo it as you need no more than a hint of the sun glinting on these areas.

4 Mix a pale orange from cadmium orange and Naples yellow. Wet the sky in places with clean water. Using a hake brush, wash the orange mixture over the left-hand side of the sky and phthalocyanine blue over the right-hand side, leaving some gaps for clouds.

5 Using the same mixtures, carry the sky colours down into the water and sand, paying careful attention to the colours of the reflections in these areas. The warm colours used in the sky and sand set the mood for the rest of the painting.

▶

6 Mix a dilute wash of pale greyish purple from cerulean blue and a little permanent rose. Wet selected areas of the sky with clean water so that the colours will merge on the paper. Using the hake brush, wash the mixture over the darkest areas of cloud on the left-hand side of the sky and bring the colour down into the background hills and water. Darken this greyish purple mixture by adding more pigment to it and start putting a little colour on the shaded side of the largest boat in the scene.

7 Using the same mixture of cerulean blue and permanent rose, continue building up washes on the sides of the largest boat.

8 Darken the harbour wall with a wash of cadmium orange mixed with Naples yellow. While still wet, drop in a mixture of phthalocyanine blue and a little raw sienna. Paint the reflections of the harbour wall in the wet sand. Apply a little cerulean blue to the main boat and the one behind it.

Tip: Do not make the wall too dark at this stage: assess how strong it should be in relation to the background.

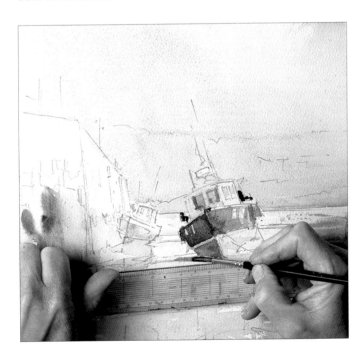

9 Using a small round brush, apply a dark mixture of ultramarine blue, burnt umber and a little cadmium red to the main boat. Mix a purplish grey from cerulean blue and permanent rose and, using a ruler or straightedge as in Step 2, paint the shadow under the main boat. Leave to dry.

10 Using your fingertips, gently rub off the masking fluid to reveal the highlights on the water and sand.

11 Apply further washes, wet into wet, over the hill in the background of the scene so that the colours fuse together on the paper, using ultramarine blue and light red, with a touch of raw sienna for the dark areas in the middle distance. Continue building up the tones of the reflections and intensify the colour of the water by adding a little cerulean blue with a touch of Naples yellow.

12 To add more texture to the ridges of sand in the foreground, apply strokes of burnt sienna straight from the tube, lightly stroking an almost dry medium filbert brush over the dry painting surface. This allows the paint to catch on the raised tooth of the paper, creating expressive broken marks that are equally suitable for depicting the sparkle of light on the water.

Assessment time

The basic structure of the painting is now in place. There are four principal planes – the sky, the landscape on the far side of the river which has put some solidity into the centre of the picture, the boat and harbour wall (the principal centre of interest in the painting), and the immediate foreground, which is structured to lead the eye up to the boat. Now you need to tie everything together in terms of tones and colours.

All the boats need to be strengthened, as they are the main interest in the painting.

The land is not sufficiently well separated from the estuary area.

More texture and depth of tone are needed on the harbour wall to hold the viewer's eye within the picture area.

▶

13 Now you can begin gradually to build up the washes to achieve the correct tonal values. Darken the harbour wall, using the original mixture of cadmium orange and a touch of raw sienna and build up the sandy area immediately in front of the main boat with the same mixture.

14 Using a small round brush and a dark mixture of ultramarine blue and light red, put in some of the detail on the boats.

15 Now concentrate on the reflections of the boats, using colours similar to those used in the original washes. Do not to make the reflections too opaque. Keep these washes watery and as simple as possible. Use vertical brushstrokes so that they look more like reflections.

16 Mix a warm blue from cerulean blue, permanent rose and a touch of burnt umber and put in the two figures and their reflections.

17 Using a fine rigger brush and resting the ferrule on a plastic ruler or straightedge, as in Step 2, put in the masts on the main boat in a mixture of ultramarine blue and light red and the rigging in a paler mixture of cerulean blue and permanent rose.

18 Using a filbert brush and the original mixture of cadmium orange and a little permanent rose, darken the stonework on the harbour wall. These uneven applications of colour give the wall texture and make it look more realistic.

Harbour moorings

This project brings together a range of classic watercolour techniques – wet into wet, building up layers of colour, using masking fluid to preserve the highlights, drybrush work – to create a lively painting that captures the atmosphere of the scene beautifully. The background is deliberately subdued in order to focus attention on the moorings. The main subject (the largest boat) is positioned at the intersection of the thirds, with the diagonal line of the sand directing the viewer's eye towards it. The different elements of the scene are perfectly balanced in terms of tone and composition.

The harbour wall is painted wet into wet to create muted but interesting colours and textures.

The town in the original scene has been replaced by an atmospheric blend of colours that suggests wooded hills.

The two walking figures introduce human interest to the scene and provide a sense of scale.

Painting Trees

It is virtually impossible to paint landscapes without painting trees as they feature heavily, even in many urban views. Trees add texture, colour and pattern, and they provide an important vertical element that often cuts startlingly across or through a work, dividing the picture area and drastically affecting the composition.

The most common mistake when painting trees is to make them all look the same. Even trees of the same species can look surprisingly different to each other, with no two trees growing in exactly the same way.

Trees are complex objects and not the easiest of things to draw or paint well. The best way to approach the subject is to simplify it, so that you paint the underlying structure and general shape of the tree before adding any detail. All trees can be seen as simple shapes which are either rounded, rectangular, columnar or pointed in their overall shape. The underlying structure is best seen in winter, when trees are devoid of leaves. The skeletal network of limbs, branches and twigs shows how the trees grow upwards and outwards from the roots and central trunk.

Although you can paint foliage as blocks of colour, you should remember that trees are composed of thousands upon thousands of delicately shaped individul leaves. Do not attempt to paint every leaf, but pay attention to the broken edge quality of the tree shape and carefully depict any spaces that you see between the leaves and branches, where the sky becomes visible.

Colour is another very important consideration. Foliage is not always green, nor are tree trunks always brown. Silver, yellow, orange, red and even purple foliage can be found, and the colour of trunks and stems can vary just as much.

A number of watercolour techniques are especially useful when painting trees. Drybrush is perfect for painting the texture on bark, as are sgraffito and linear marks made using a pencil or a fine brush. Broken colour techniques are particularly successful for foliage: try using natural sponges to gently dab a second colour over dry washes.

Winter trees ▼
The initial scene was established using wet-into-wet washes. Once these had dried, further washes were applied to bring out the intricate forms and pattern of the crossing jumble of gnarled branches and the shadows they cast across the trunk. The shadow of the tree seen coming in from the bottom of the picture is a compositional device, indicating that things do not end at the picture edge.

Autumn beech tree ▼

The fine linear textures on the trunk of this beech tree were made by applying masking fluid with a pen. The same technique was used for some of the fine branches.

The foliage colour was flooded on using orange, yellows and browns applied wet into wet, while the foliage texture was achieved by sprinkling rock salt onto the wet paint.

Cedar tree ▶

This delicate painting carefully observes the way the branches spread and fall in layers around the thick central trunk. Painted using a fine brush and wet-on-dry washes, the foliage colours consist of only three tones of the same silver-green colour.

Tips: • Study the tree's growth habit and break it down into a simple basic shape. Establish the overall shape of the tree before adding surface detail.
• Use drying marks where paint has puddled and dried at different speeds to suggest clumps of foliage.
• Experiment with textural techniques like wax resists, sponging, and using rock salt.
• Instead of using colours straight from the paint box, mix greens and other tree colours: the results will look far more natural and subtle.

Woodland in spring

Green is, without any doubt, the most important colour in the landscape artist's paint palette. Once you start to look, it is astonishing how many different shades there are, from the bright, almost acidic greens of fresh spring growth through to muted tones of olive and sage.

Although a quick glance through any paint manufacturer's catalogue will reveal a wide range of ready-made greens, it is quite unusual to find one that suits your needs exactly, and you almost always have to modify commercial colours or mix your own. This project, of a spring woodland in the late-afternoon sunlight, gives you the opportunity to do precisely that.

So that you build on what you learn here, make a point of painting different types of woodland: a coniferous forest, for example, tends to contain darker greens than the deciduous woodland shown here. It is a good idea to keep a note of the paint colours used in successful colour mixes so that you can easily recreate them at a later date.

The time of year makes a difference, too. At the height of summer, you will find that leaves are larger and darker than they are in spring, and the tree canopy is more dense, making it harder for light to penetrate through to the woodland floor. In a deciduous woodland in winter, on the other hand, the trees will have lost their leaves and so it will be much easier to see the underlying shapes and structure of different tree types.

The direction and angle of the light also affects the shade of green: the same leaves can look completely different in colour depending on whether the sun is to one side or behind. A single back-lit leaf, with the veins clearly visible, can make an interesting watercolour study in its own right.

Materials
- *2B pencil*
- *90lb (185gsm) rough watercolour paper, pre-stretched*
- *Watercolour paints: cadmium red, yellow ochre, lemon yellow, alizarin crimson, phthalocyanine blue, cobalt blue, raw umber*
- *Brushes: Chinese*

The original scene
This photograph captures the essence of the scene – the slender trees and dappled light – but there is no real focus of interest. The artist decided to make one tree more prominent by bringing it forwards. This breaks the straight line across the centre of the image and allows the viewer's eye to weave in and out of the trees.

The trees form a straight line across the picture and appear to merge together.

Bright, wide shafts of sunlight indicate that the tree canopy is not very dense.

1 Using a 2B pencil, lightly sketch the scene, putting in the trunks of the main trees and indicating some of the clumps of grass alongside the track.

2 Mix a pale golden brown from cadmium red and yellow ochre. Using a Chinese brush, loosely brush the mixture on to the trunks of the main foreground trees and the pebbly track to establish the warm undertones of the painting. Mix a pale wash of lemon yellow and brush it over the foliage area as a base colour, leaving some gaps for where the brightest patches of sky show through. Add a little more pigment to the wash as you get closer to ground level, as not as much light reaches this area. Brush the same lemon yellow wash loosely over the clumps of grasses in the foreground. Leave to dry.

3 Mix a warm purplish grey from alizarin crimson and phthalocyanine blue and brush it over the shaded areas of the track. Paint the tree trunks with the same mixture. Mix a warm brown from yellow ochre and cadmium red and paint the larger stones on the track. Using a 2B pencil, lightly sketch in the leaf masses on the trees.

5 Mix a dark green from lemon yellow and phthalocyanine blue and paint the grasses growing under the trees, using short vertical strokes.

4 Mix a cool green from lemon yellow and cobalt blue and brush in the mid-tone foliage areas. Take care not to obliterate all the very lightest foliage areas that you applied in Step 2, otherwise you will lose the feeling of dappled light and fresh spring growth in the image.

Tip: When painting foliage and grasses, try to make your strokes follow the direction of growth.

▶

6 Add more phthalocyanine blue to the mixture and dab it over the foliage for the darkest greens. Strengthen the tree trunks, using the same grey mixture as in Step 3. Mix a dark brown from phthalocyanine blue, alizarin crimson and raw umber, and paint the shaded sides of the tree trunks, cutting in and out of the foliage masses.

7 Put in the darker tones of the main foreground tree, using the same mixture. Mix a bright, dark green from phthalocyanine blue and raw umber and dot in the darker foliage tones on the foreground trees. It is important to have more detail in the foreground, as it is closer to the viewer, while impressionistic blurs will suffice in the background.

Assessment time
The woodland scene is beginning to take shape but the details are still relatively indistinct and much more needs to be done to separate the foreground elements from the background. When you move on to the next stage, make sure you don't concentrate on one area at the expense of the rest. Work across the painting as a whole, standing back every now and then to assess the tonal values and compositional balance.

8 Strengthen the shadow colour on the track, using the same alizarin crimson and phthalocyanine blue mixture as before. Add more alizarin crimson and put in some thin trunks on the left of the painting. Using a blue-biased mixture of alizarin crimson and phthalocyanine blue, start dotting in some dark pebbles on the track.

The foreground shadows need to be strengthened to enhance the feeling of dappled light coming through the trees.

The background is all of a similar tone. As a result, there is not a strong enough sense of depth in the image.

The main tree is beginning to stand out from the background, but more detail is still needed here.

9 Some of the foliage areas look very light. Dot in a mid-toned green to tone down the brightness a little.

Woodland in spring

With its bright, fresh greens and dappled light, this painting is suffused with a wonderful feeling of spring sunlight. The painter has used a little artistic licence to make the composition more dynamic than it was in real life: one tree has been placed at the intersection of the thirds to provide a focus of interest, and the straight line of trees has been staggered in order to encourage the viewer's eye to move around the whole picture.

Soft, pale colours and a lack of detail imply that this area of the scene is further away from the viewer.

Long shadows lead the viewer's eye through the scene and indicate low-angled afternoon sunlight.

Crisp leaf detail helps to separate this tree from those in the background, where the foliage is much less distinct.

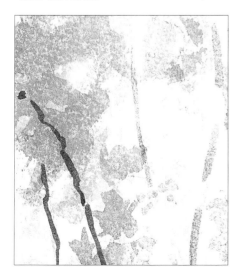

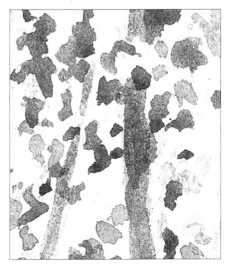

Autumn tree

Many trees are at their most dramatic in the autumn, when the leaves change from green to dazzling displays of reds, russets and golds. Combine those colours with early-morning mists, as in this scene, and you will have the makings of a very atmospheric painting.

When you are painting trees, always start by establishing the overall shape. The oak tree in this project has a spreading habit: the branches radiate outwards from the main trunk, while the crown is rounded and reasonably symmetrical. When trees are in leaf the underlying "skeleton" can sometimes be hidden from view, but you need to be aware of it. The leaves do not simply sit on top of the branches in clumps; they are attached to branches and twigs, and you must convey a sense of the shapes underneath and the directions in which the branches and twigs grow, even if you cannot see them clearly, in order for your painting to look convincing.

Because the sunlight in this scene is coming from behind the tree, the tree itself is in semi-silhouette. However, the light does catch the edge of the tree branches in places, creating warm wisps of colour against the dark branches and trunk. Pay careful attention to these highlights and look for areas where shafts of sunlight break through.

Textures, too, are important. Although you cannot see much detail because the tree is in semi-silhouette, the gnarled trunk is an essential part of the tree's character. Here, water-soluble pencils were used to establish a base texture that was then overlaid with watercolour washes.

Materials

- *4B pencil*
- *140lb (300gsm) NOT watercolour paper, pre-stretched*
- *Water-soluble pencils: sepia*
- *Watercolour paints: cadmium yellow, burnt sienna, alizarin crimson, cobalt blue, sepia, violet*
- *Gouache paints: neutral grey, permanent white*
- *Brushes: medium round, small round*
- *Ruling drawing pen*
- *Masking fluid*

Preliminary sketch
The artist made a quick colour sketch in situ to work out the overall shape of the tree and which colours to use for the vibrant autumn leaves.

1 Using a 4B pencil, lightly sketch the scene, putting in the main branches of the tree. Look carefully at how they twist and overlap.

2 Dip the tip of a sepia water-soluble pencil in water and put in the dark textural markings of the gnarled trunk and the main branches. (Dipping the pencil in water intensifies the colour and makes the marks more permanent, so that this linear pencil work is still visible when the watercolour washes are applied to the tree in the later stages of the painting.)

3 Using a ruling drawing pen, apply masking fluid to the highlighted edges of the branches and the foreground grasses. Leave to dry completely. The masking is subtle, but it plays an important role in establishing a sense of light and shade.

4 Mix a pale wash of cadmium yellow and wash it over the background behind the tree and the foreground grasses. Dot some of the same cadmium yellow mixture into the branches to establish the lightest-coloured foliage areas.

5 Wet the tree with clean water and touch in burnt sienna, dabbing it on with the side of the brush. The colour will spread over the damp paper and merge with the yellow applied in Step 4. Apply several layers wet into wet, in some places, to deepen the tones.

6 While the burnt sienna washes are still wet, drop alizarin crimson into the lower branches, angling your brushstrokes in the direction in which the branches and leaves naturally grow. The richness of the autumnal colours is now starting to develop. Leave to dry.

7 Wash around the edges of the tree and into the negative spaces with clean water. Mix a very pale, dilute grey from neutral grey gouache and cobalt blue watercolour and touch this mixture on to the damp paper. Add a tiny amount of burnt sienna to the mixture and paint the misty tree trunks in the background, wet into wet.

8 Mix a greyish brown from burnt sienna, sepia and a tiny amount of cobalt blue. Paint the branches of the main tree, looking carefully to see which branches go behind others. Even though you are brushing over the water-soluble pencil marks made in Step 2, they will show through again once the watercolour wash is dry.

▶

Assessment time

The main colours have been established but it is hard to tell which direction the light is coming from, and without any strong indication of light and shade, the tree looks rather flat and one-dimensional. For the remainder of the painting, concentrate on improving the tonal contrast and creating a feeling of sunlight streaming through the tree branches.

There needs to be more tonal contrast on the trunk, in particular, to make the tree look natural and rounded.

Foreground detail is essential in order to make the tree look as if it is standing on solid earth.

9 Brush loose strokes of burnt sienna into the foreground, bringing some of your strokes up over the yellow grasses. The warm colour and foreground texture help to bring this area of the painting forward. Leave to dry completely. Using your fingertips, gently rub off the masking fluid to reveal the highlighted edges of the branches and the foreground grasses. The feeling of light and shade in the painting is now much stronger.

10 Mix a pale grey from white gouache, cobalt blue and violet and paint the exposed areas of the branches and trunk. Spatter alizarin crimson on to the leaves. Leave to dry.

11 Mix a very pale yellow from permanent white gouache with a little cadmium yellow. Brush in very thin shafts of misty early-morning sunlight.

Autumn tree

Painted in a free and spontaneous manner, this little study exploits the richness of autumn colours to the full. In any subject that is viewed against the light, the detail is subdued: here, the dense browns of the trunk and branches provide the necessary structure for the painting, while virtually everything else is reduced to an impressionistic mass of colour. The semi-opaque yellow mixture used to create the shafts of sunlight mutes the underlying colours but does not obscure them completely. This is a very effective way of creating the effect of early-morning mist.

The misty trees in the background provide a hint of the landscape beyond.

Water-soluble pencil marks convey the texture of the tree bark beautifully.

Spattering provides the merest hint of leaf texture: too much would be distracting.

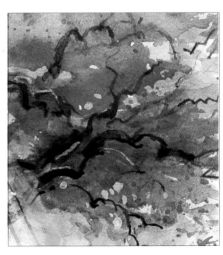

Poppy field

Lush expanses of wild flowers are always attractive, and when those flowers are a rich and vibrant red, like this stunning array of poppies, the subject simply cries out to be painted.

This project presents you with several challenges. First and foremost, it is an exercise in painting spontaneously and in creating an impression of the scene, rather than trying to capture each individual flower. Work quickly and freely, and concentrate more on the overall tones than on specific details. Make sure you don't make the poppies look as if they have been planted in neat, straight rows. It is surprisingly difficult to position dots of colour randomly, but unpredictable techniques, such as spattering, can help.

Second, remember that this is not a botanical study: what you are trying to create is an overall impression of the scene, not an accurate record of how the flowers are constructed. You really don't want a lot of crisp detail in a scene like this, otherwise it will look stilted and lifeless. This is where watercolour really comes into its own. Wet-into-wet washes that merge on the paper create a natural-looking blur that is perfect for depicting a mass of flowers and trees gently blowing in the breeze.

Finally, take some time considering the tonal balance of the painting. Red and green are complementary colours and they almost always work well together, but if the greens are too dark they could easily overpower the rest of the painting. On the other hand, if they are too light they will not provide a strong enough backdrop for the flowers.

Materials
- *2B pencil*
- *140lb (300gsm) rough watercolour paper, pre-stretched*
- *Watercolour paints: cobalt blue, alizarin crimson, gamboge, raw sienna, sap green, Delft or Prussian blue, burnt umber, viridian, cadmium orange, cadmium red, Payne's grey*
- *Brushes: large mop, medium mop, fine rigger, old brush for masking fluid, medium round, fine round*
- *Masking fluid*

The original scene
This field is a blaze of red poppies as far as the eye can see, counter-balanced by a dark green background of trees. Although the horizon is very near the middle of the picture, which can sometimes makes an image look static, this is offset by the fact that the top half of the image is divided more or less equally into trees and sky. However, the sky is very bright, and this detracts from the poppies; adding colour here will improve the overall effect.

The sky lacks colour and needs to be made less dominant.

The dark trees provide a neutral background that makes the red of the poppies all the more vibrant.

1 Using a 2B pencil, lightly sketch the outline of the trees and some of the larger foreground poppies. Don't attempt to put in every single flower – a few of the more prominent ones are all you need as a guide at this stage. Using an old brush, apply masking fluid over the poppies in the foreground. In the middle ground and distance, dot and spatter masking fluid to create a more random, spontaneous effect. Draw some thin lines of masking fluid for the long grasses in the foreground. Clean your brush thoroughly and leave the painting to dry.

2 Using a medium round brush, dampen the sky area with clean water, leaving a few strategically placed gaps for clouds. Mix up a strong wash of cobalt blue and drop this on to the damp sky area, so that it spreads up to the gaps left for the cloud shapes. The colour is more intense than it was in reality, but the sky needs to look dramatic. Leave to dry.

3 Apply a strong wash of gamboge to the tree tops. Add raw sienna and brush over the base of the trees and the horizon. Touch raw sienna into the clouds. While this is still damp, touch a purplish-blue mixture of cobalt blue and alizarin crimson on to the underside of the clouds. Leave to dry.

4 Mix a dark green from sap green, raw sienna and a little Delft or Prussian blue. Using a medium round brush, brush this mixture over the trees to create dark foliage areas, allowing some of the underlying gamboge to show through in places.

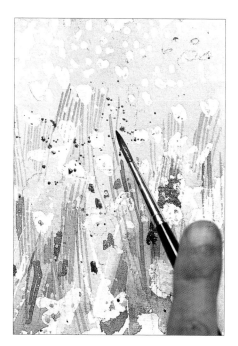

5 Continue building up the foliage on the trees, leaving a few gaps. Mix a mid-toned green from gamboge and sap green and, using a large mop brush, brush this mixture over the lower part of the painting – the poppy field. Leave to dry.

6 Mix a darker green from viridian and cobalt blue and apply this mixture to the foreground, using a large mop brush. Use the same colour to touch in some dark lines for the long shadows under the main tree. Leave to dry.

7 Mix a dark green from sap green, raw sienna and burnt umber and, using a fine rigger brush, brush thin lines on to the foreground. Leave to dry. Spatter the same mixture over the foreground to represent the grass seed heads and add texture. Leave to dry.

▶

Assessment time

Cool greens and yellows have been put in across the whole painting, establishing the general tones of the scene. As you continue to work, you will probably find that you need to darken some of the background colours to maintain a balance between them and the foreground. This kind of tonal assessment should be an on-going part of all your paintings. Now it is almost time to start putting in the bright red poppies in the foreground, the finishing touches that will bring the scene to life. Try above all else to maintain a feeling of spontaneity in the painting as you work: the poppies must look as if they are randomly distributed over the scene.

The dark tonal masses of the background have been established.

Spattering in the foreground gives interesting random texture.

8 Mix a dark green from Delft or Prussian blue, viridian and burnt umber and, using a medium mop brush, darken the trees, leaving some areas untouched to create a sense of form. Add a little more burnt umber to the mixture and, using a fine rigger brush, paint the tree trunks and some fine lines for the main branches. Leave to dry. Using your fingertips, gently rub off the masking fluid.

9 Mix an orangey red from cadmium orange and cadmium red. Using a fine round brush, start painting the poppies in the background.

10 Continue painting the white spaces with the red mixture used in Step 11, leaving a few specks of white to give life and sparkle to the painting. Apply a second layer of colour to some poppies while the first layer is still wet; the paint will blur, giving the impression of poppies blowing in the wind, and the tone will deepen.

11 Using a fine, almost dry brush and the same dark green mixture used in Step 7, paint in the exposed foreground stalks and grasses. Finally, using a fine rigger brush, touch in the black centres of the poppies with a strong mixture of Payne's grey.

Poppy field

This is a loose and impressionistic painting that nonetheless captures the mood of the scene very well. It exploits the strong effect of using complementary colours (red and green), but the density of colour has been carefully controlled so that the whole painting looks balanced, with no one part dominating the rest.

The sky is darker than in the original photograph, which helps to maintain the tonal balance of the scene.

The shadow under the tree is painted with short brushstrokes that echo the direction in which the grasses and flowers grow.

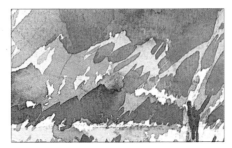

Only the foreground poppies have painted centres. Those in the background are so far away that a blur of colour suffices.

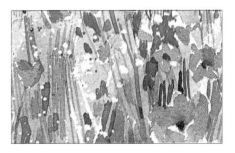

Painting Flowers

The aim of botanical artists is to record for scientific purposes. They need to create as faithful a representation of the flower or plant as possible, with every detail in evidence. The so-called fine artists usually paint flowers for decorative and symbolic reasons, and, of course, because flowers and plants make such terrific subjects.

Like other subjects, you should start by looking at and understanding the basic shape of the flowers you are painting. Look at how they grow and at how the leaves are attached to the stem and radiate out from it. Remember that the flower or flowers are an extension of the stem and not simply something that is stuck on the end of it. The flower head is made up of several different parts: note how each is connected to the others.

Analysing and reducing these often complex elements into simple geometric shapes is a good way to start. Look closely and you will see that flower heads can resemble saucer-like discs, simple spheres, upright or inverted cones, bell or goblet shapes, to name but a few. Learning to look at flowers in this way will not only allow you to draw and paint them well, but it will also let you approach the subject in a looser, more impressionistic or expressionistic way, secure in the knowledge that you are capturing the character of your subject correctly.

You can use every watercolour technique in your repertoire when painting flowers, but planning the sequence in which you are going to work is essential. Unless you are using body colour, you will be working from light to dark, and this often raises the question of how to paint small, complex-shaped flowers against a dark background without painstakingly painting around each flower. (The answer is, of course, masking fluid.)

The colour of certain flowers can seem particularly elusive, as can the way in which colours often bleed into each other, or are distributed on the petals. Make your colour mixes a little stronger and more intense that you think they should be, as watercolour always looks paler when it is dry. Use wet-into-wet techniques, as these will allow the colours to run and mix together by themselves.

◄ **Pansies**
This colourful painting uses several watercolour techniques. The image was blocked in using wet-into-wet washes of transparent watercolour. Body colour was then added, some of which was removed by carefully blotting with a paper towel. Detail was added using more body colour and soft pastel.

Parrot tulips ▼

Wet-into-wet and wet-on-dry wash techniques were used to paint these parrot tulips. Chance back-runs and drying marks add to the pattern and interest on the leaves and flower heads, while the characteristic curve of the stems under the weight of the flower heads has been perfectly captured.

Spring bouquet ▶

Here, irises, tulips, anemones and small yellow narcissi have been painted in their wrapping paper. Although the arrangement looks casual, it was very carefully arranged. Wet-on-dry washes were used exclusively. The colours were kept bright by using no more than three layers of wash in any one place.

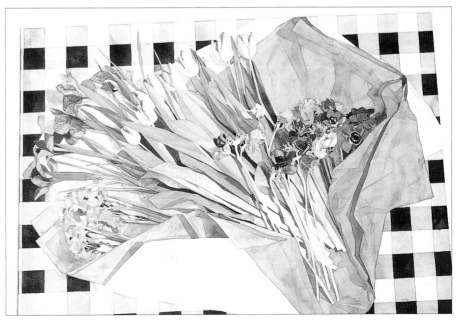

Tips: • Look at the underlying structure and simplify what you see into basic geometric shapes.
• Make several studies of your subject before you begin painting, to increase not only your technical skills, but also your familiarity with the subject.

58

Sunflower

Bold and bright, their faces turning to
follow the sun as it travels through the
sky, sunflowers are an artist's dream.

Although the aim of this project is not
to produce a botanical illustration, with
every last detail precisely rendered, a good
flower "portrait" should show something
of how the flower is constructed. Is the
stem straight or twisted? Are the leaves
grouped together at the base of the stem
or spread out evenly? Does the flower
consist of a single large bloom or lots of
little florets? A side view will often tell you
more than a face-on viewpoint and can
make it easier to make the flower look
three-dimensional, particularly when you
are painting a relatively flat, symmetrical
flower, such as a sunflower.

Materials
- 4B pencil
- 140lb (300gsm) NOT watercolour
  paper, pre-stretched
- Oil pastels: orange, lemon yellow,
  bright yellow, sage green, light green,
  burnt sienna
- Watercolour paints: burnt sienna,
  violet, cadmium yellow, yellow
  ochre, Hooker's green, cobalt blue,
  cerulean blue
- Gouache paints: permanent white
- Brushes: medium round

The set-up
Because sunflowers were not in bloom
when this painting was done, an
artificial sunflower was used for the
composition. The stem and flowerhead
have been twisted slightly to make the
image more interesting.

Reference photograph
The artist used a photograph as reference for the colours and the texture in the
flower centre. However, the head-on viewpoint and frontal lighting do not make
a very interesting composition as there are virtually no shadows or changes of tone
in the petals.

1 Angle the sunflower so that you can
see both the interior of the flower
and the backs of some of the petals.
Using a 4B pencil, lightly sketch the
sunflower, paying careful attention
to the way the leaves are twisted.

2 Begin putting in some detail with oil
pastels, which will act as a resist and
allow you to make short, textural marks
that would be difficult to achieve using
a brush alone. Use orange in the flower
centre, lemon yellow and bright yellow
on the lightest parts of the petals, and
sage and light green on the stalk.

3 Continue using the oil pastels on the stalk and leaves, using sage for the shadowed side of the stalk and the deepest creases in the leaves and light green for the other leaf markings and highlights.

4 Mix a mid-toned wash of burnt sienna watercolour paint and brush it over the centre of the flower. Mix a dark brown from burnt sienna and violet and paint the darkest part of the flower centre.

5 Mix a mid-toned wash of cadmium yellow and brush it all over the flower. While this first wash is still wet, mix a light brown from yellow ochre and burnt sienna and drop it wet into wet on to the inner petals, allowing some of the underlying yellow to show through as striations in the petals.

6 Mix a mid-toned green from Hooker's green with a little yellow ochre and begin brushing in the colour for the leaves. Add more yellow ochre to the mixture for the top leaf, which is slightly withered. Note how the oil pastel markings show through from beneath the watercolour.

7 While this first green wash is still wet, continue painting the leaves. Sunflower leaves are very textured, so paint the deep crinkles in the main leaf, wet into wet, in cobalt blue, using the tip of the brush. This foreground texture helps to imply that the leaf is closer to the viewer than the others.

▶

8 Paint the base petals around the outer edge of the flower in a light green mixture of Hooker's green and cadmium yellow. Paint the lowest leaf on the left in the same green mixture used in Step 6, adding cerulean blue to the mixture for the top edge. This cool colour helps to make the leaf recede. Brush yellow ochre, wet into wet, on to the outer edge of this leaf.

Assessment time
The use of warm and cool tones in the leaves is beginning to make the spatial relationships clearer. The cool blue-green of the leaf to the left of the stalk makes it recede, while the warmer greens and yellow ochre of the leaf immediately below the flower make it advance, implying that it is closer to the viewer. Although the painting is nearing completion, some subtle adjustments need to be made in order to create more texture and build up the tones.

More variety of tone is needed on the petals.

The two lowest leaves are too similar in tone: the one at the base needs to be very slightly darker, so that it comes forward more.

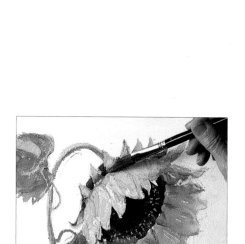

9 Enhance the feeling of light and shade by painting the shadowed side of the stalk in cobalt blue. Dot more blue in behind the base petals.

10 Darken the petals and add texture to the inside of the flower, which is shaded from the light, by dotting in orange oil pastel.

11 Dash short strokes of burnt sienna and yellow oil pastel on to the inner petals in order to darken the tones still further.

Sunflower

This is a colourful and lively flower study that captures the essence of the plant. Note how wet-into-wet washes create subtle variations in tone on both the flower and the leaves, while the use of oil resists provides interesting textures and highlights. Angling the head of the sunflower and positioning the stalk on a slight diagonal have also helped to create a dynamic composition.

Using pale tones and leaving some of the white paper still visible indicate that this area receives the most direct light.

Oil pastel markings create important tonal and textural contrasts in the centre of the flower.

The shadow cast by the leaf above helps to define the spatial relationships of the leaves.

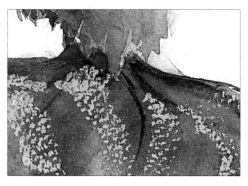

Summer flower garden

This scene was invented entirely from the artist's imagination, using quick sketches of flowers in her own garden and photographs from a garden centre catalogue as reference. When you are combining material from several sources, take the trouble to check a few basic facts. Make sure that the flowers you've selected really do bloom at the same time, and check the relative sizes, so that you don't make a ground-hugging plant appear taller than a small tree.

The project gives you the chance to combine classic watercolour techniques with the relatively modern medium of water-soluble pencils. The characteristics of water-soluble pencils are exploited to the full here. The pencil marks are used dry, to create fine linear detail, particularly in the foreground. They are also covered with watercolour washes, so that the colours merge. You can control the amount of blur to a certain extent: if you wet the tip of the pencil before you apply it, the pencil marks will blur less, allowing you to hold some of the detail and texture in these areas.

Materials
- *140lb (300gsm) NOT watercolour paper, pre-stretched*
- *Water-soluble pencils: dark blue, light brown, cerulean blue, light violet, dark violet, blue-green, olive green, red, yellow, orange, deep red, green*
- *Watercolour paints: cerulean blue, rose doré, Linden green, dark olive, olive green, cobalt blue, cadmium yellow, Naples yellow, burnt sienna, vermilion, alizarin crimson, Payne's grey*
- *Brushes: medium round, fine round*
- *Ruling drawing pen*
- *Masking fluid*

Tip: Changing from a horizontal to a vertical format may alter other elements as well. In the final composition, the path still runs from the bottom right to the top left but the artist made the foreground flower border more prominent.

Reference sketches
Look closely at detailed sketches, illustrations or photographs of individual flowers before you embark on your full-scale painting. Although a massed clump of foliage and flowers may look like an indistinct jumble, knowing the shape and colour of an individual bloom will help you capture the essential features of the plant.

Preliminary sketch
The artist invented a garden scene and made a small sketch to try out the colours and the composition. To begin with, she opted for a horizontal format. Then she decided that this placed too much emphasis on the pathway and that a vertical format, with the rose arch as the main feature, would have more impact.

1 Using a dark blue water-soluble pencil, sketch the main shapes of your subject. Dip a ruling drawing pen in masking fluid and mask the lightest parts of the flowers.

2 One of the advantages of using a ruling drawing pen is that it holds the masking fluid in a reservoir. A range of marks is used to convey the different textures of each of the massed clumps – flowing lines for the poppy heads and little dashes for the daisy petal in the foreground. It would be more difficult to achieve this with a dip pen as the nib would block up, leaving blobs and blots on the paper.

3 Shade in the trunk of the tree with loose pencil strokes, using a light brown water-soluble pencil. (This makes the marks more permanent.) Dip the tip of the pencil in clean water and draw the branches. Draw the wooden rose arch in the same colour. Colour in the individual delphinium blooms with small dots of cerulean blue, changing to light and dark violet for the stems that are in deeper shade. Dip the pencil tip in water to make some of the marks.

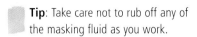
Tip: Take care not to rub off any of the masking fluid as you work.

Assessment time
Continue with these dots and dashes of pencil work until you have established the general colour scheme of the garden. Don't be tempted to do too much or the pencil work might begin to overpower the picture: this is a painting, not a drawing, and it is the watercolour paint applied in the subsequent stages that will give the work its character.

Blue-green for the foliage.

Olive green and light violet for the iris leaves.

Yellow, red and orange for the poppies.

The negative spaces between the clumps of flowers are as important as the flowers themselves.

4 Dampen the background with water. Wash a pale mix of cerulean blue watercolour paint over the sky, brushing around the branches. Dot rose doré over the rose arch: the paint will blur, suggesting full-blown blooms. Brush Linden green under the arch and dot a mixture of dark olive and cerulean blue into the background and between the delphiniums. While the paint is still damp, add bright olive green with cerulean blue and brush over the first blue wash.

5 Dampen the middle distance with clean water. Dot cerulean blue, rose doré and cobalt blue on to the delphiniums. Both the paint and the initial water-soluble pencil marks will blur and spread, causing the flowers to look slightly out of focus. Mix a neutral brown from olive green and rose doré and brush it into the negative spaces between the iris stems. The flowers will begin to stand out more against this dark background.

6 The distance and middle ground have now been established. Note how the soft tones and lack of clear detail help to imply that these areas are further away from the viewer.

7 Mix a bright green from cerulean blue and cadmium yellow and dot it loosely into the pathside area for the hummocks of low-growing ground-cover plants that spill over on to the path.

8 Dampen the path. Starting near the arch, brush pale Naples yellow over the path, adding burnt sienna towards the foreground. Brush clean water over the tip of a brown water-soluble pencil and spatter colour on to the path, using the brush. Start spattering in the foreground and work towards the rose arch. As the brush dries, the drops of water – and the dots of colour – get smaller, and this will help to create a sense of recession.

9 Note how effectively the curved path leads the eye to the focal point of the painting – the rose-covered arch. The spattered drops of colour provide important texture in what would otherwise be a large expanse of flat brown.

10 Brush cadmium yellow and then vermilion over the red poppy heads, allowing the colours to blend on the paper, and brush a tiny bit of alizarin crimson over parts of the foreground poppies to give added depth of tone.

11 Mix Payne's grey with olive green for some of the background poppy leaves and stems. Add a little cobalt blue to the mixture for the foreground poppy leaves. Dot cadmium yellow in the centre of the daisy flowers.

▶

12 Finish the bottom left-hand corner, using the same green mixture as before.

13 Using your fingertips, gently rub off the masking fluid to reveal the white parts of the flowers.

14 Some of the exposed white areas now look too stark – particularly in the background. Mix a very pale wash of cerulean blue and brush it over some of the iris stems to tone down the brightness – otherwise the viewer's eye will be drawn to these areas, which are not the most important parts of the scene.

15 Now go back to the water-soluble pencils to add sharper details in the foreground. Use a deep red pencil to delineate the petals and frilly edges of some of the larger poppies, and draw a green pencil circle around the yellow centres of the poppies. Darken the spaces between the daisy petals with a dark blue pencil.

Summer flower garden

This painting is a romantic, impressionistic portrayal of a traditional flower garden. Softly coloured poppies, irises, daisies and delphiniums line the winding path, which leads to the focal point of the image – the rose arch. There is a hint of mystery in the painting, too: what lies on the other side of the archway?

Flowers in the background are more blurred than those in the foreground, but some linear detail is still visible.

The poppies are painted with a number of different techniques – masking for the twisting stems, wet-into-wet washes for subtle colour blends, and fine pencil detail.

Reserving the white of the paper for the daisy petals adds sparkle to the image.

The textured path provides subtly coloured but necessary foreground interest.

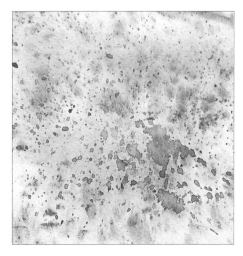

French vineyard

This deceptively simple-looking scene is a useful exercise in both linear and aerial perspective. Take care over your underdrawing, as it underpins all the rest of the painting: if the rows of vines appear to be going in the wrong direction it will look very strange. It is worth taking plenty of time over this stage.

You also need to mix tones carefully. Note how the dark green vine leaves in the foreground give way to a much paler, yellower green in the distance – and then see how these pale greens gradually darken again above the horizon line, shifting from a mid green to a very bluish green on the distant hills. Remember to test out each tone on a scrap piece of paper before you apply it to the painting.

Materials
- *2B pencil*
- *140lb (300gsm) rough watercolour paper, pre-stretched*
- *Watercolour paints: cerulean blue, Naples yellow, gamboge, light red, sap green, ultramarine violet, cobalt blue, viridian, Payne's grey, burnt umber*
- *Brushes: large mop, medium mop, fine round*

Reference photographs
Sometimes one reference image simply doesn't give you enough information to create the painting you want. Don't be afraid to combine elements from several photos or sketches to create the desired effect. Here, the artist referred to the long panoramic-format photograph for the close-up detail of the vine leaves and the farm buildings, but based his composition on the larger photograph, in which the rows of vines are angled in a more interesting way.

1 Sketch the outline of the hills and vines, then dampen the sky with clean water, leaving some gaps. Mix a wash of cerulean blue and drop it on to the damp areas. Leave to dry.

2 Mix a pale wash of Naples yellow and touch it into the dry cloud shapes and along the horizon line. Leave to dry.

3 Darken the top of the sky with cerulean blue and leave to dry. Mix gamboge with light red and brush over the vines. Paint light red on the foreground and in between the vines.

4 Using a medium mop brush, loosely paint sap green into the foreground to indicate the rows of vines. Leave to dry.

5 Mix a deep blue from ultramarine violet, cobalt blue and viridian and wash it over the hills. Put a few dots along the top edge to break up the harsh outline and imply trees.

6 Mix a mid-toned green from viridian with a little cobalt blue. Using a medium mop brush, brush this mixture over the lower part of the hills. Mix a dark blue from cobalt blue, ultramarine violet and viridian. Using a large mop brush, darken the shadows on the distant hills. Use the same colour to stipple a few dots on the green hills to imply trees on the horizon.

Tip: It is often easier to assess colours if you turn your reference photo upside down. This allows you to concentrate on the tones without being distracted by the actual subject matter.

Assessment time

Once you are happy with the general lines and colours of the scene, you can start thinking about adding those all-important touches of detail and texture. Don't be tempted to do this too early: once you have painted the detail, it will be much harder to go back and make any tonal corrections to the background or the spaces between the rows of vines.

The perspective of the foreground has been established, leaving you free to add detail and texture.

The background is virtually complete, with darker shadows on the hills providing a sense of light and shade.

7 Mix a dark green from sap green, Payne's grey, and a little burnt umber. Using a large mop brush, wet the foreground with clean water, leaving gaps for the vines. Using a medium mop brush, brush the dark green mixture on to the damp areas and let it flow on the paper to define the general green masses of the vines and their leaves. Paint the dark shapes of the foreground vine leaves.

8 Continue painting the vine leaves, as in Step 7. Don't try to be too precise or the painting may easily start to look overworked: generalized shapes will suffice. Mix a warm but neutral grey from ultramarine violet and burnt umber and, using a fine round brush, paint in the stems of the vines and the posts that support them, taking care to make the posts smaller as they recede into the distance.

9 Mix a dark shadow colour from ultramarine violet and a little burnt umber and brush this mixture across the ground in between the rows of vines. Again, take care over the perspective and make the shadows narrower as the vines recede into the distance.

10 Mix a warm, reddish brown from light red and a touch of Naples yellow and use this to paint the buildings in the background. This warm colour causes the buildings to advance, even though they occupy only a small part of the picture area. Using a fine brush and the same dark green mixture that you used in Step 7, touch in some of the detail on the vines.

11 Using an almost dry brush held on its side, brush strokes of light red in between the rows of vines. This strengthens the foreground colour but still allows the texture of the paper to show through, implying the pebbly, dusty texture of the earth in which the vines are planted.

12 Using a fine brush, brush a little light red on the top of the roofs. This helps the roofs to stand out and also provides a visual link with the colour of the earth in the foreground. Add a little burnt umber to the light red mixture to darken it, and paint the window recesses and the shaded side of the buildings to make them look three-dimensional.

French vineyard

Fresh and airy, this painting is full of rich greens and warm earth colours, providing a welcome dose of Mediterranean sunshine. Note how most of the detail and texture are in the foreground, while the background consists largely of loose washes with a few little dots and stipples to imply the tree-covered mountains beyond. This contrast is a useful device in landscape painting when you want to establish a sense of scale and distance.

Cool colours in the background recede.

Simple dots and stipples are enough to give the impression of distant trees.

Note how the rows of vines slant inwards and converge towards the vanishing point.

Warm colours in the foreground advance.

Craggy mountains

This project is a good exercise in aerial perspective. Although the scene itself is very simple, you must convey a sense of the distances involved in order for it to look convincing. Tonal contrast is one way of achieving this: remember that colours are generally paler towards the horizon, and so the mountains in the far distance look paler than those in the immediate foreground. Textural contrast is another way to give a sense of distance: details such as jagged rocks and clumps of snow need to be more pronounced in the foreground than in the background.

The use of warm and cool colours to convey a sense of light and shade is important, too. Cool colours, such as blue, appear to recede and so painting crevices in the rocks in a cool shade makes them look deeper and further away from the viewer. Warm colours, on the other hand,

appear to advance and seem closer to the viewer. These should be used for the areas of rock that jut upwards into the sunlight.

Although you want the painting to look realistic, don't worry too much about capturing the exact shapes of individual rocks: it is more important to convey an overall impression. Use short, jagged strokes that follow the general direction of the rock formations. This will help to convey the mountains' craggy texture.

The original scene

These craggy peaks, stretching far into the distance, make a dramatic image in their own right. In the late spring, when this photograph was taken, the drama is enhanced by the billowing white clouds, set against a brilliant blue sky, and the last vestiges of snow clinging to the rocks.

Materials

- *2B pencil*
- *Rough watercolour board*
- *Watercolour paints: ultramarine blue, burnt sienna, cobalt blue, phthalocyanine blue, alizarin crimson, raw umber*
- *Brushes: large round, old brush for masking*
- *Sponge*
- *Tissue paper*
- *Masking fluid*
- *Scalpel or craft (utility) knife*

Tip: The sponge is used in this project to lift off paint colour applied to the sky area, and to apply paint. The surface of the sponge leaves a soft, textured effect.

Textural detail is most evident in the foreground; this also helps to create a sense of distance.

Note how the colours look paler in the distance, due to the effect of aerial perspective.

1 Using a 2B pencil, lightly sketch the scene, indicating the main gulleys and crevices and the bulk of the clouds in the sky. Keep your pencil lines loose and fluid: try to capture the essence of the scene and to feel the "rhythm" of the jagged rock formations.

2 Mix a pale, neutral grey from ultramarine blue and burnt sienna. Using a large round brush, wash this mixture over the foreground mountain.

3 Mix a bright blue from cobalt blue and a little phthalocyanine blue. Using a large round brush, wash it over the top of the sky. While this is still wet, dampen a small sponge in clean water, squeeze out the excess moisture, and dab it on the sky area to lift off some of the colour. This reveals white cloud shapes with softer edges than you could achieve using any other technique.

Tip: Each time you apply the sponge, turn it around in your hand to find a clean area, and rinse it regularly in clean water so that you don't accidentally dab colour back on to the paper.

▶

4 Mix a neutral purple from alizarin crimson, ultramarine blue and a little raw umber. Using a large round brush, dampen the dark undersides of the clouds and touch in the neutral purple mixture. While this is still damp, touch in a second application of the same mixture in places to build up the tone. If necessary, soften the edges and adjust the shapes of the dark areas by dabbing them with a piece of sponge or clean kitchen paper to lift off colour.

5 Study your reference photograph to see exactly where the little patches of snow lie on the foreground mountain. Using an old brush, apply masking fluid to these areas to protect them from subsequent applications of paint. Use thin lines of fluid for snow that clings to the ridges and block in larger areas with the side of the brush. Wash the brush in liquid detergent and warm water. Leave the masking fluid to dry completely before moving on to the next stage.

6 Mix a dark blue from cobalt blue and phthalocyanine blue and paint the distant hills between the two mountains. Dilute the mixture and brush it over the background mountain. Leave to dry. Mix a dark brown from burnt sienna with a little alizarin crimson and ultramarine blue, and wash this mixture over the background mountain. Add a little alizarin crimson and begin painting the foreground mountain.

7 Using a large round brush, continue to paint the foreground mountain. Use the same dark brown mixture that you used in Step 6 for the areas that catch the sun, and phthalocyanine blue for the areas that are in the shade. Paint with relatively short and slightly jagged vertical brushstrokes that echo the direction of the rock formations. This helps to convey the texture of the rocks.

Assessment time
Because of the careful use of warm and cool colours, the painting is already beginning to take on some form. Much of the rest of the painting will consist of building up the tones you have already applied to enhance the three-dimensional effect and the texture of the rocks. At this stage, it is important that you take the time to assess whether or not the areas of light and shade are correctly placed. Note, too, the contrast between the foreground and the background: the foreground is more textured and is darker in tone, and this helps to convey an impression of distance.

The rocks that jut out into the sunlight are painted in a warm brown so that they appear to advance.

The crevices are in deep shade and are painted in a cool blue so that they appear to recede.

The background mountain is painted in a flat colour, which helps to convey the impression that it is further away.

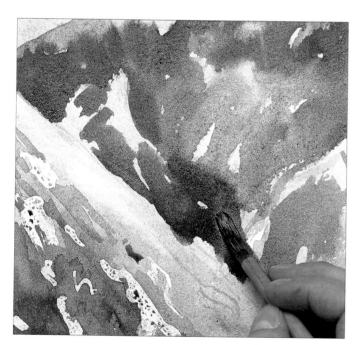

8 Mix a deep, purplish blue from alizarin crimson, phthalocyanine blue and raw umber. Brush this mixture along the top of the background peak, leaving some gaps so that the underlying brown colour shows through. Using the dark brown mixture used in Step 6, build up tone on the rest of the background mountain, applying several brushstrokes wet into wet to the darker areas.

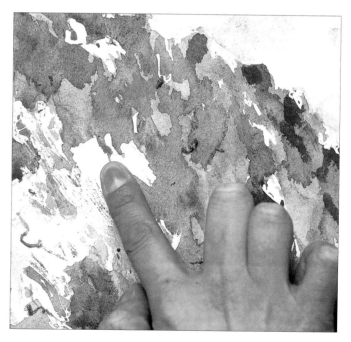

9 Continue building up the tones on both mountains, using the same paint mixtures as before. Leave to dry. Using your fingertips, gently rub off the masking fluid to reveal the patches of white snow. (It is sometimes hard to see if you've rubbed off all the fluid, so run your fingers over the whole painting to check that you haven't missed any.) Dust or blow all dried fluid off the surface of the painting.

▶

10 Using the tip of a scalpel or craft (utility) knife and pulling the blade sideways, so as not to cut through the paper, scratch off thin lines of paint to reveal snow in gulleys on the background mountain.

11 Apply tiny dots of colour around the edges of some of the unmasked areas to tone down the brightness a little. Continue the tonal build-up, making sure your brushstrokes follow the contours of the rocks.

12 Dip a sponge in clean water, squeeze out any excess moisture and dampen the dark clouds. Dip the sponge in the neutral purple mixture used in Step 4 and dab it lightly on to the clouds to darken them and make them look a little more dramatic.

13 The final stage of the painting is to assess the tonal values once more to make sure that the contrast between the light and dark areas is strong enough. If necessary, brush on more of the purplish blue mixture used in Step 8 to deepen the shadows.

Craggy mountains

This is a beautiful and dramatic example of how contrasting warm colours with cool colours can create a sense of three dimensions. Although the colour palette is restricted, the artist has managed to create an impressively wide range of tones.

Jagged brushstrokes that follow the direction of the rock formations create realistic-looking textures on the foreground mountain and the white of the paper shines through in places, giving life and sparkle to the image.

The white of the paper is used to good effect to imply patches of snow clinging to the rocks.

The soft-edged clouds and brilliant blue sky provide a perfect counter-balance to the harshness of the rocks below.

The background mountain is painted in flat washes, with far less textural detail than the foreground.

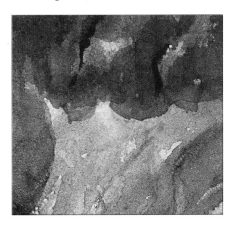

Painting Still Lifes

Of all the subjects to draw and paint, still lifes are unique as all the elements are under your control – not only the objects being used, but also their position and the quality and direction of the light used to illuminate them. This gives you the chance to work at your leisure, with no pressure, and to experiment with composition, colour and technique.

Still-life subjects are found everywhere. The obvious ones include the numerous and ever-increasing varieties of fruit, vegetables and flowers available all year round. Kitchen and gardening equipment, children's toys, ceramics and glassware, patterned fabrics, found natural objects and the numerous objets d'art that litter most homes: the list is endless.

Traditionally, the objects used in a still life have some kind of association with each other, but you can also make interesting images by grouping together a range of objects that have little, or no, common ground.

There are also what are known as "found" still lifes, which are arrangements that you simply come across by chance. By definition, these are usually less contrived and more natural-looking than an arranged grouping. Found groupings might include fruit and vegetables falling out of a shopping basket, or a group of terracotta flower pots and garden tools in the corner of a shed or outbuilding.

Perhaps the most important point to consider with still lifes is the quality or type of light that you use to illuminate your subject. Although natural light is ideal, it can prove problematic. Arranging still-life groups directly in the sun can make for dramatic, strong images, but the sun will move and the light will constantly change. You can use lamps of various kinds to light your subject. It is important to remember that low-voltage bulbs can give an orange cast, so it is better to invest in a few daylight bulbs, as these will make colours look cleaner and brighter.

Tips: • Invest in a couple of anglepoise lamps and daylight bulbs, so that you can control the direction and quality of the light.
• Make a series of thumbnail sketches of the composition before you begin. Often, you will find that a better composition suggests itself.
• Take risks with your groupings and compositions in order to give your images an edge.
• Look out for "found" groupings that may give rise to an image. If you do not have painting materials to hand, capture the moment with a photograph.

Tulips ▼
Natural sunlight pours through a window and falls on a bunch of tulips. The intensity of the light is exaggerated by making the shadow on the wall much darker than it was in reality.

Pumpkins ▲
This painting was made on a heavy, rough paper that did not require stretching. Gum arabic was used in the mixes to increase the intensity and transparency of the paint. The paint was applied wet into wet and wet on dry, and areas of paint were removed and distressed using abrasive paper.

Leeks ▶
This is a contrived and carefully arranged still life. The leeks and knife are viewed from above, and an illusion of depth is achieved by painting the linear pattern on the cloth at a slight angle.

80

Strawberries and cherries in a bowl

Still lifes don't have to be complicated, and with a few colourful fruit and a china bowl, you can set up a simple but very attractive study on a corner of your kitchen table. However, you do need to spend time thinking about your composition: with relatively few elements, the position of each one is critical.

When you have chosen your subject, move the fruit and bowl around until you get an arrangement that you are happy with. Look at the shadows and the spaces between the objects, as well as at the objects themselves: they are just as important in the overall composition.

Above all, this is an exercise in colour. Choose fruit that have some variation in colour, to provide visual interest. Also look for complementary colours – ones that are opposite each other on the colour wheel – such as red and green, or yellow and violet. Here, touches of green on the leaves and stems offset the vibrant reds of the fruit, while shadows on the yellow ochre background are painted in a complementary shade of violet.

Remember that even things that you know are a brilliant white, such as the doily on which the bowl stands, should rarely (if ever) be painted as such. Shadows and reflected light imbue them with a subtle but definite hue of another colour. Half close your eyes to help you assess what colours and tones to use, and keep any washes in these areas very pale to begin with. You can build them up later if necessary, but if you make them too strong there's no going back.

Materials
- *2B pencil*
- *140lb (300gsm) NOT watercolour paper, pre-stretched*
- *Watercolour paints: yellow ochre, dioxazine violet, cobalt blue, Hooker's green, vermilion, cadmium orange, cadmium red, cerulean blue, cadmium yellow, Naples yellow, alizarin crimson, leaf green, olive green, phthalocyanine blue*
- *Brushes: medium chisel*
- *Ruling drawing pen*
- *Masking fluid*

The set-up
Set up your still life on a plain white piece of paper, so that you can concentrate on the subject, and position a table lamp to one side to cast interesting shadows. Experiment by placing the fruit in different positions and at different angles: you need to create a balanced composition so that you don't end up with too large an area of empty background.

The strawberries shade gradually from deep red to a pale yellow.

The bowl is painted in strong colours that detract from the fruits.

1 Using a 2B pencil, lightly sketch the fruit and the bowl and roughly indicate the cut-paper pattern on the doily.

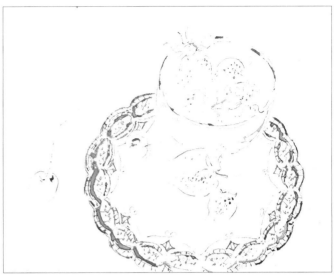

2 Dip a ruling drawing pen in masking fluid and mask out the areas that will be left white in the final painting – the bright highlights on the fruit and the rim of the bowl and the pattern on the doily.

3 Finish off the masking. You must leave it to dry completely before you start to apply any paint, otherwise you run the risk of smudging it and destroying the crisp, clean lines that you want to keep.

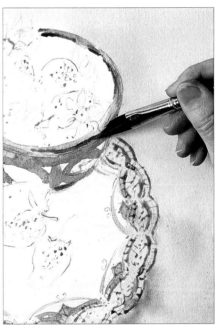

4 The white background is very stark, so start by mixing yellow ochre with a little dioxazine violet to make a dull yellow as a background colour. Dampen the background and the patterned edge of the doily with clean water, taking care to brush around the cherry, and brush the mixture over this area, adding a little more violet to the mixture on the left-hand side. Brush a slightly darker violet under the edge of the doily to create a slight shadow. The background and shadow colours are virtually complementary colours, which work well together.

5 Mix a dull blue from cobalt blue and a little dioxazine violet. Using the tip of the brush, start to paint the blue of the pattern on the bowl. Continue to build up the pattern, using Hooker's green and a pale mixture of vermilion and a little dioxazine violet.

> **Tip**: Make the colours on the bowl more subdued than they are in real life, so that they do not detract from the vibrant reds of the fruit.

▶

6 Mix a rich orange from cadmium orange and cadmium red and finish painting the pattern on the bowl. Mix a very pale blue from cobalt blue and cerulean blue and paint the inside of the bowl, taking care not to touch any of the fruit. Brush a little dioxazine violet into the most deeply shaded part of the inside of the bowl. Leave to dry.

7 You need to work quickly for the next two stages, which are painted wet into wet so that the colours merge on the paper. Mix a very pale yellow from cadmium yellow and a hint of Naples yellow. Wet the strawberries with clean water and carefully brush this yellow mixture on to the palest areas, taking care not to allow any paint to spill over on to the doily.

8 While this is still damp, mix cadmium red with a little cadmium orange and brush this mixture over the red parts of the strawberries. Mix vermilion with alizarin crimson and drop this mixture wet into wet on to the very darkest parts of the strawberries. (You may need several applications to build up the necessary density of tone.)

9 Paint the cherry on the background in vermilion. Apply another layer of vermilion while the first one is still wet, brushing a little cadmium yellow on to the right-hand side to give some variety of tone. Mix alizarin crimson with a hint of dioxazine violet and paint the cherry on the doily, which is a darker tone than the one on the background. Leave to dry.

10 Brush clean water over the strawberry leaves. Paint the lightest leaf areas in cadmium yellow, the mid tones in leaf green, and the darkest tones in olive green, adding a little phthalocyanine blue to the olive green for the very shaded parts.

Assessment time

Paint the cherry stalks in olive green and darken the tone of the leaves overall, if necessary. The painting is very nearly complete, but you need to build up the shadows to make the still life look more realistic. Study your subject carefully to work out where the shadows fall and how dark they need to be in relation to the rest of the painting.

Subtle variations in tone across the surface of the fruit help to make them look lifelike.

Even though the doily is very thin, the lighting is so strong that it should cast a definite shadow.

With no shadows to anchor them, the cherries and strawberries look as if they are suspended in mid-air.

11 Brush clean water over the doily, carefully brushing around the fruit and bowl. Mix a very pale wash of cerulean blue and brush it over the doily; the paint will blur and spread softly, without leaving any harsh edges. While this wash is still damp, mix a very pale purple from dioxazine violet with a tiny amount of Hooker's green and paint the shadows under the fruit and bowl, wet into wet. Use the same paint mixture to brush in the shadow under the background cherry, this time wet on dry.

12 Although one is painted wet into wet and one wet on dry with harsher edges, the shadows under the two cherries look equally effective.

> **Tip**: Using a very pale wash of colour over the doily prevents it from looking too stark and bright, and helps to highlight the intricate patterning.

13 Deepen the shadow under the doily, using the same purple mixture of dioxazine violet and Hooker's green as used in Step 11. Leave to dry.

14 Using your fingertips, gently rub off the masking fluid, revealing the brilliant white of the doily and the highlights on the fruit and bowl.

Strawberries and cherries in a bowl

This is a simple, yet carefully thought out, still life in which rich colours and textures abound. Note, in particular, the effective use of complementary colours. The artist has put together an attractive arrangement in which the shadows and the spaces between the objects play as important a role in the overall composition as the objects themselves.

The intricate pattern and brilliant white of the doily are preserved through the careful application of masking fluid.

The reds are achieved by carefully building up a number of different tones – cadmium red, vermilion and alizarin crimson.

The colours of the bowl are deliberately subdued, so as not to detract from the richly coloured fruit.

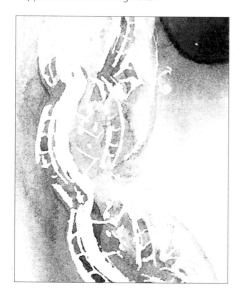

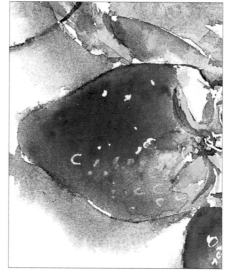

Still life with stainless steel

This kind of still life project is easy to set up at home. The trick is not to make the composition too complicated: a few colourful objects, strategically placed to exploit the way they are reflected in the metallic surfaces, will suffice.

Although this looks, at first glance, like a relatively simple still life, it requires very careful assessment of tone. Metal objects and other reflective surfaces take a lot of their colour from the objects that are reflected in them, so in this project you will need to look carefully at the reflections in order to assess what colours and tones you need to apply. However, the reflections tend to be a little more subdued in tone and less crisply defined than the objects being reflected. Bear this in mind while you are working and adjust your paint mixtures accordingly.

It is a common mistake to paint reflective surfaces too light, with the result that they lack substance. Remember to assess the tones of your painting at regular intervals and build up the tones gradually until the density is right.

Another aspect of tone that you need to consider here is how to make your subject look three-dimensional. To give form to a subject, you need to put darker tones on the shadowed side, but when you are dealing with curved or spherical shapes, like the stainless steel olive oil pourers in this project, the curves are so smooth that it can be hard to decide where the darker colours should begin. Work wet into wet for these areas, so that the colours merge naturally on the paper without any hard edges.

Materials
- 2B pencil
- 200lb (425gsm) NOT watercolour paper, pre-stretched
- Watercolour paints: cerulean blue, Payne's grey, cadmium lemon, ivory black, raw umber, burnt umber, lamp black, yellow ochre, burnt sienna, dioxazine purple, cadmium orange, alizarin crimson
- Brushes: fine round, medium round
- 2B graphite stick

The set-up
When you are setting up a still-life that contains shiny, reflective surfaces, make sure that the light source (which, indoors, is invariably some kind of lamp) does not reflect too prominently in the subject. The best way to do this is to place the light source to one side and at a reasonable distance from your subject.

1 Using a 2B pencil, lightly sketch the outline of your subject, making sure the shapes are accurate. You may find it easier to assess the shapes objectively if you turn your drawing upside down.

2 Mix pale washes of cerulean blue, Payne's grey, cadmium lemon and ivory black. Using a fine round brush, start to paint the lightest tones on the stainless-steel olive oil pourers, leaving any highlights as white paper. Judge which colour to use where by looking carefully at the reflections.

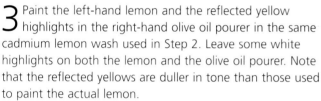

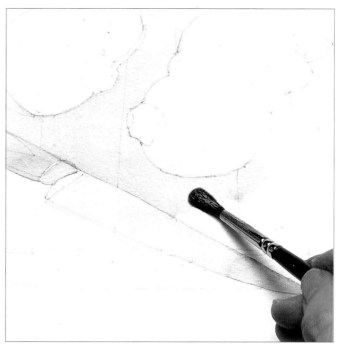

3 Paint the left-hand lemon and the reflected yellow highlights in the right-hand olive oil pourer in the same cadmium lemon wash used in Step 2. Leave some white highlights on both the lemon and the olive oil pourer. Note that the reflected yellows are duller in tone than those used to paint the actual lemon.

4 Paint the two right-hand lemons in the same pale cadmium lemon wash. Mix a mid-toned brown from raw umber with a touch of burnt umber and paint the handle of the knife. Paint the blade of the knife in a very dilute wash of lamp black, leaving a highlight near the handle. Leave to dry. Mix a pale brown from yellow ochre and a little burnt sienna and, using a medium round brush, paint the wooden chopping board.

Assessment time
The initial, lightest washes have now been laid down and the base colours of the whole still life established. You can now begin to elaborate on this, building up tones to the correct density and putting in the details. Work slowly, building up the tones gradually to avoid the risk of laying down a tone that is too dark.

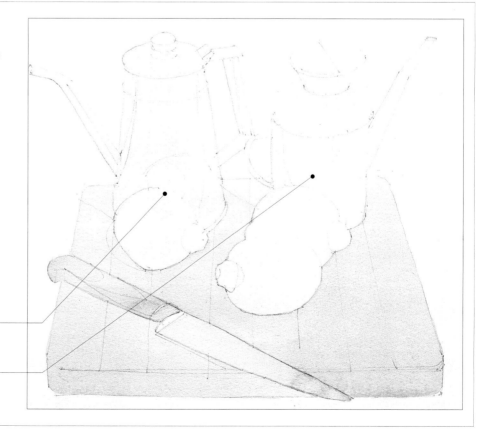

The very brightest highlights have been left as white paper.

The reflections are muted in colour and worked wet into wet so that the colours blur a little.

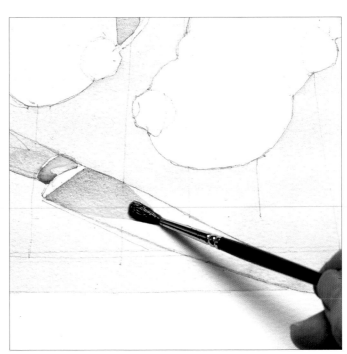

5 Mix slightly darker versions of the greys and blues used in Step 2, adding a touch of dioxazine purple to the cerulean blue, and start to paint in the mid tones on the olive oil pourers, gradually defining the individual facets more clearly. Leave to dry.

6 Mix a mid-toned grey from Payne's grey and ivory black and darken the blade of the knife, leaving an area of lighter tone near the handle. Make sure you don't go outside the pencil lines: the outline of the knife must be crisply defined. Leave to dry.

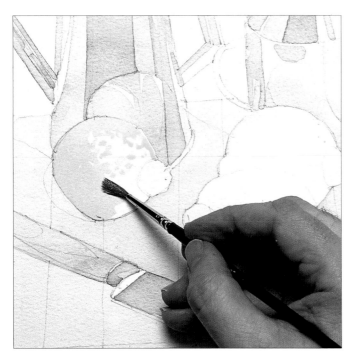

7 Add cadmium lemon to the mixture used to paint the chopping board in Step 4 and paint the reflections of the lemon in the pots. Begin to intensify the colour on the lemons themselves with a wash of cadmium lemon, working around the highlights. As you work down the lemons, gradually add cadmium lemon and then a hint of cerulean blue to the mixture, so that the colour is darker on the shadowed underside and the rounded shape of the fruit is clearer.

8 Touch a little more greenish yellow into the reflections of the lemons. Paint the handle of the knife again with the same mixture of raw umber and burnt umber used in Step 4, leaving a slight gap in the middle, where light hits the edge, to indicate the change of plane between the side and top of the handle. Leave to dry. All the mid tones of the painting have now been established.

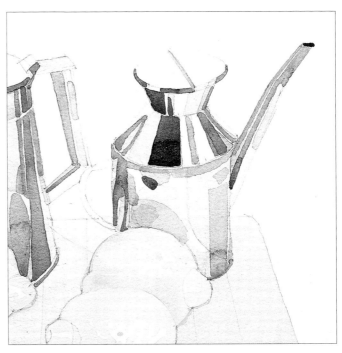

9 Mix slightly darker versions of the greys and blues used in Step 5 and continue reinforcing the tones on the olive oil pourers. As you darken these tones, the reflections (which are considerably lighter in colour) will begin to stand out even more clearly.

10 Strengthen the tones of the right-hand olive oil pourer in the same way, paying careful attention to the different facets of the two pourers. Add a touch of cadmium orange to paint the reflection of the chopping board.

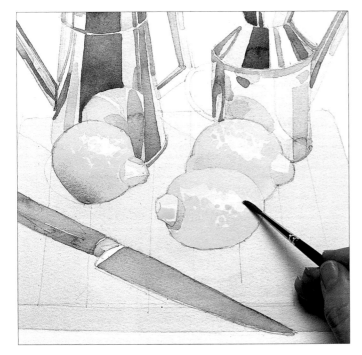

11 Using the same yellow mixtures as used in Step 7, build up the density of tone on the lemons. Again, remember to work carefully around the highlights that you left white in Step 3. Leave to dry.

12 Mix a dark brown from burnt umber and burnt sienna and, using a fine round brush, carefully paint the shaded side of the knife handle under the highlight line, making sure you retain the crisp, sharp lines. The knife immediately looks much more three-dimensional. Leave to dry. Using the same fine round brush, stipple a little of the greenish yellow mixture on to the dark undersides of the lemons to create the pitted surface texture of the fruit.

▶

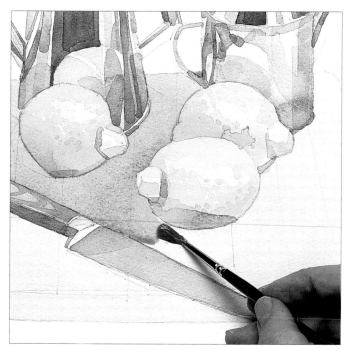

13 In these final stages of the painting, put in the very darkest tones. Work across the painting as a whole, assessing the tones in relation to each other rather than concentrating on one specific area.

14 Brush a little more of the greenish yellow mixture on to the underside of the foreground lemon. Leave to dry. Using the dark brown mixture of burnt umber and burnt sienna, and a medium round brush, paint the top of the chopping board. Leave to dry.

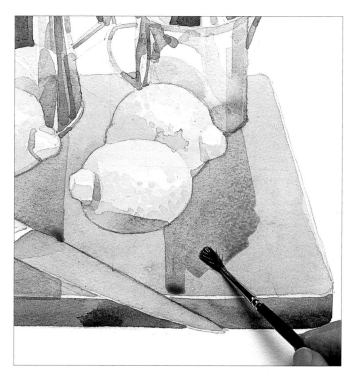

15 Darken the burnt umber and burnt sienna mixture by adding a little more burnt sienna and a hint of alizarin crimson. Paint the front of the chopping board, which is in shadow, leaving a tiny highlight along the edge between the top and front of the board. Leave to dry. Paint alternate panels on the top of the board in a mixture of burnt umber and burnt sienna. Leave to dry.

16 Add a little dioxazine purple to the dark brown mixture that you used to paint the front of the chopping board and paint the shadows behind the olive oil pourers and under the lemons and the knife. Leave to dry. Using a 2B graphite stick, draw vertical lines on the chopping board to indicate the grain of the wood.

Still life with stainless steel

This is a contemporary-looking still life with bold shapes and shadows. All the elements are contained within a triangle formed between the tip of the knife and the spouts of the olive oil pourers. Placing the knife on the diagonal also makes the composition more dynamic. Several layers of colour are applied to build up the tones to the right density.

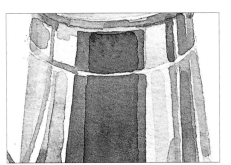

Variations in tone convey the shape of the olive oil pourers.

The reflections are slightly blurred and more subdued in tone that the objects being reflected.

Simple pencil lines effectively convey the grain of the wooden board without detracting from the main subjects.

Eye of the tiger

People sometimes say that the eyes are the windows of the soul and, regardless of whether you are painting humans or animals, they certainly tell you a lot about the character and mood of your subject. All too often, eyes are drawn and painted as circles or ovals, which looks very unnatural. The eyeball is spherical even though, of course, only a small part of it is visible. This spherical shape is particularly obvious if you look at an eye from the side, but regardless of your viewpoint it helps to think of the eye as a three-dimensional form.

Subtle blends of colour are essential when it comes to painting the iris of the eye, while the "white" of the eye is often shadowed and not white at all. Finally, you must capture that all-important sparkle, which makes your subject look alive. Look at the position and shape of bright highlights in the eyes.

The artist chose a tiger's eye for this demonstration, because he also wanted to explore the markings on the surrounding fur, but the same principles apply to all subjects. An original painting of a tiger was used as reference material.

Materials
- *HB pencil*
- *Hot-pressed watercolour board or paper*
- *Watercolour paints: cadmium yellow, cadmium red, burnt sienna, Payne's grey, viridian, French ultramarine, Vandyke brown, ivory black*
- *Gouache paints: permanent white*
- *Brushes: fine round, ultra-fine round*

1 Using an HB pencil, lightly sketch the tiger's eye on smooth watercolour board or paper. Mix cadmium yellow with cadmium red for the gold of the eye and apply it carefully, using a fine round brush. Leave to dry. Mix burnt sienna with a little cadmium yellow and brush it over the tiger's fur, leaving the highlight area under the eye untouched. Paint the black facial markings around the eye in a dark mixture of Payne's grey. Leave to dry.

2 Mix a cool green from viridian and a little French ultramarine and, using a fine round brush, brush it over the top half of the iris, covering the pupil. Leave to dry. The basic colours and shapes have now been established. The next stage is to make the eye look three-dimensional by showing how the lids curve over the eyeball.

3 Using an ultra-fine round brush, paint the upper part of the iris in Payne's grey, gently feathering the colour down on to the green. This softens the transition in colour from one part of the eye to the next and looks much more natural than hard-edged, concentric circles of colour. Darken the upper rim of the eye with Payne's grey. Leave to dry.

4 Darken the markings around the eye with a mixture of Vandyke brown and Payne's grey. Paint the pupil in the same colour.

5 While the pupil is still damp, feather the colour down on to the iris, so that there is a very subtle transition of colour. Mix French ultramarine with a touch of permanent white gouache and, using a fine round brush, brush in the shaded areas of the fur, making sure your brushstrokes follow the direction of the fur growth. Build up the dark markings around the eye with ivory black. Leave to dry.

6 Continue to build up the dark markings around the eye with ivory black. Darken the brown fur colour with burnt sienna and Vandyke brown, alternating between the two. Add tiny strokes of permanent white gouache on the eyeball and the lower eyelid to create highlights.

Eye of the tiger

The dramatic colouring and fine detail make this a very attractive study. Subtle feathering of colour and the careful positioning of the highlights on both the eyeball and the lower lid combine to depict a rounded and very life-like eye. Tiny details like this can have as much impact as a full-scale painting and are a good way of practising difficult subjects.

Tiny touches of permanent white gouache on the pupil reflect the light, while subtle feathering softens the transition from one colour to the next.

Although the fur is white, it is in shade here and is painted in pale French ultramarine.

Tabby cat

Cat fur is fascinating to paint and you will find a huge variety of markings, from tortoiseshell and tabby cats with their bold stripes to sleek, chocolate-point Siamese and long-haired Maine Coons. One of the keys to painting fur is being able to blend colours in a very subtle way, without harsh edges. Even pure white or black cats, with no obvious markings, have their own "patterns": because of reflected light and shadows, the fur of a pure white cat will exhibit clear differences in tone which you need to convey in your paintings.

Fur markings also reveal a lot about the shape of the animal. You need to look at an animal's fur in much the same way as a portrait painter looks at how fabrics drape over the body of a model: changes in tone and in the direction of the fur markings indicate the shape and contours of the body underneath. Always think about the basic anatomy of your subject, otherwise the painting will not look convincing. If you concentrate on the outline shape when you are painting a long-haired cat, for example, you could end up with something that looks like a ball of fluff with eyes, rather than a living animal. The cat in this project has relatively short hair, which makes it easier to see the underlying shape.

Cats seem to spend a lot of their time sleeping or simply sprawled out, soaking up the sunlight and, if you are lucky, you might have time to make a quick watercolour sketch. For "action" pictures – kittens batting their paws at a favourite toy or adult cats jumping from a wall or stalking a bird in the garden – you will almost certainly have to work from a photographic reference. You will be amazed at the number of ways cats can contort their bodies.

Materials
- *HB pencil*
- *140lb (300gsm) rough watercolour paper, pre-stretched*
- *Watercolour paints: yellow ochre, raw umber, alizarin crimson, ultramarine blue, cadmium red, Prussian blue, burnt sienna*
- *Gouache paints: Chinese white*
- *Brushes: medium round, fine round*

Reference photograph
This is a typical cat pose – the animal is relaxed and sprawled out, but at the same time very alert to whatever is happening around it. The markings on the fur are subtly coloured but attractive. The face is full of character, and this is what you need to concentrate on in your painting. If you can get the facial features to look right, you are well on the way to creating a successful portrait.

A plain background allows you to concentrate on the subject.

The eyes, the most important part of the portrait, are wide open and alert.

1 Using an HB pencil sketch the cat, making sure you get the angle of the head right in relation to the rest of the body. Start with the facial features, sketching the triangle formed by the eyes and nose, then work outwards. This makes it easier to position the features in relation to each other. If you draw the outline of the head first, and then try to fit in the facial features, the chances are that you will make the head too small.

2 Mix a pale wash of a warm brown from yellow ochre and raw umber. Using a medium round brush, wash the mixture over the cat leaving the palest areas, such as the insides of the ears and the very light markings, untouched.

3 Add a little more raw umber to the mixture to make a darker brown and paint the darker areas on the back of the head and back.

4 Continue applying the darker brown mixture, which gives the second tone. You are now beginning to establish a sense of form in the portrait.

5 Add a little alizarin crimson and ultramarine blue to the mixture to make a dark, neutral grey. Begin brushing in some of the darker areas around the head.

▶

6 Add more water to the mixture and paint the cat's back, which is less shaded. Start painting some of the markings on the hind quarters, using short, spiky brushstrokes along the top of the cat's back. This indicates that the fur does not lie completely flat.

7 Mix a warm brown from yellow ochre and raw umber and brush it loosely over the mid-toned areas. Mix a warm pink from alizarin crimson and a little yellow ochre and, using a fine round brush, paint the insides of the ears, the pads of the paws, and the tip of the nose.

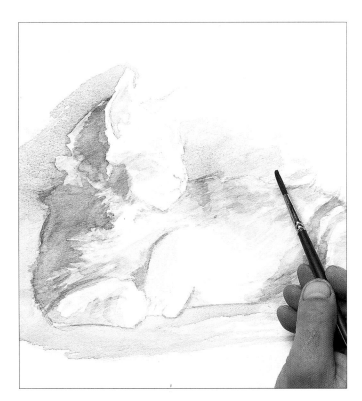

8 Mix a warm maroon colour from cadmium red, yellow ochre and alizarin crimson and paint the surface on which the cat is lying. Add ultramarine blue to darken the mixture and paint the background, carefully brushing around the cat.

9 Mix a purplish blue from ultramarine blue and cadmium red. Using a fine round brush, paint the dark fur on the side of the cat's head, the nostril, the area under the chin and the outline of the eye.

Assessment time

Although the broad outline of the cat is there, along with some indication of the markings on the fur, the painting does not yet look convincing because the body looks flat rather than rounded. In addition, the cat's head is merging into the warm colour of the background, when it needs to stand out much more clearly.

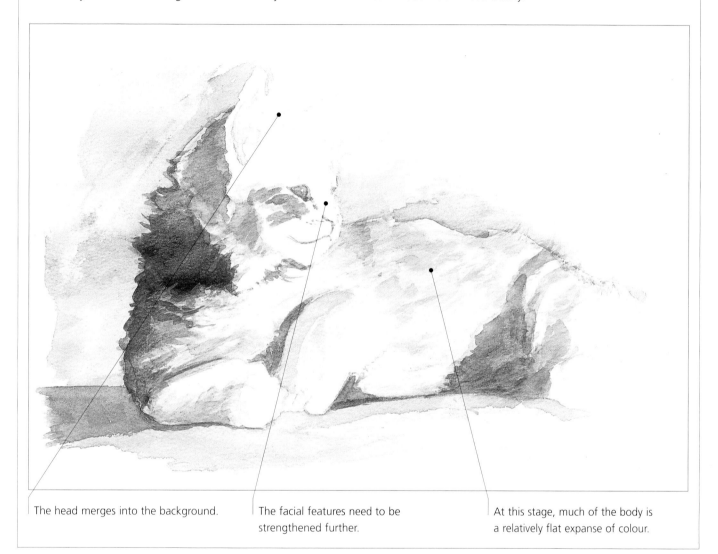

The head merges into the background.

The facial features need to be strengthened further.

At this stage, much of the body is a relatively flat expanse of colour.

10 Mix a greenish black from Prussian blue, burnt sienna and cadmium red and paint the pupil of the eye, leaving a white highlight. Brush more of the purplish-blue mixture used in Step 9 on to the shaded left-hand side of the cat and strengthen the shadow under the chin and on the back of the cat's head.

Tip: Pay careful attention to the highlight in the cat's eye. The shape and size of the white area must be accurate in order to look lifelike.

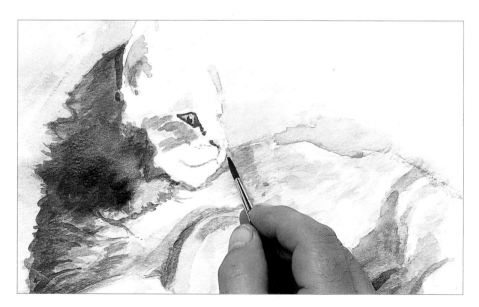

11 Using the same purplish-blue mixture, put in some of the stripes on the hind quarters and darken the tones on the back, paying careful attention to the direction of the brushstrokes so that the markings follow the contours of the body.

12 Using the same mixture, continue darkening the tones on the back to give a better sense of form.

13 Adjust the tones where necessary. Now that you have put in lots of darks, you may need to tone down some of the bright areas that have been left unpainted by applying a very dilute wash of the first pale brown tone.

14 Darken the insides of the ears with alizarin crimson. Using a very fine brush and Chinese white gouache, paint the whiskers.

Tabby cat

This is a lively and engaging study of a favourite family pet. All portraits, whether they are of humans or animals, need to convey the character of the subject. The artist has achieved this here by placing the main focus of interest on the cat's face and its alert expression. The fur is softly painted, with careful blends of colour, but the markings are clearly depicted.

The facial features are crisply painted.

Deep shadow between the paws helps to create a sense of depth in the painting.

The markings change direction, following the contours of the body beneath.

Otter

This delightful study of an otter, peering inquisitively out to sea, is an exercise in building up textures. You can put in as much or as little detail as you wish, but don't try to finish one small area completely before you move on to the next. Go over the whole painting once, putting in the first detailed brushmarks, and then repeat the process as necessary.

Remember to work on a smooth, hot-pressed watercolour paper or board when using masking film (frisket paper). If you use masking film on a rough-surfaced paper there is a risk that the film will not adhere to the surface properly, allowing paint to slip underneath and on to the area that you want to protect. Smooth paper also enables you to make the fine, crisp lines that are essential in a detailed study such as this.

Materials

- *HB pencil*
- *Hot-pressed watercolour board or smooth paper*
- *Watercolour paints: ultramarine blue, cadmium yellow, burnt sienna, Vandyke brown, Payne's grey, cadmium red*
- *Gouache paints: permanent white*
- *Brushes: medium flat, medium round, fine round, very fine round*
- *Masking film (frisket paper)*
- *Scalpel or craft (utility) knife*
- *Tracing paper*

Reference photographs
Here the artist worked from two reference photographs – one for the otter's pose and fur detail, and one for the seaweed-covered rocks in the foreground. When you do this, you need to think carefully about the direction of the light. If you follow your references slavishly, you may find that sunlight appears to hit different areas of the picture at different angles, which will look very unnatural.

Preliminary sketches
Quick pencil sketches will help you to select the best composition, while a watercolour sketch is a good way of working out which colours to use.

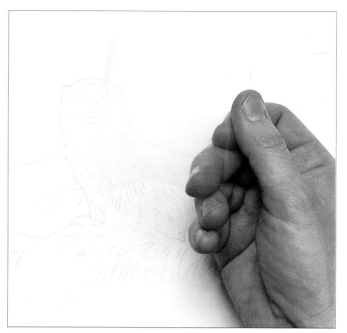

1 Using an HB pencil, copy your reference sketch on to watercolour board or smooth paper. Place masking film over the picture area. Using a sharp scalpel or craft (utility) knife, cut around the otter and rocks. To avoid damaging your painting surface, trace your pencil sketch, then place the masking film over the tracing paper, cut it out, and reposition the film on the painting surface.

2 Carefully peel back the masking film from the top half of the painting. You may need use a scalpel or craft knife to lift up the edge. You can now work freely on the sky and background area, without worrying about paint accidentally spilling over on to the otter or foreground rocks – though it is worth rubbing over the stuck-down film with a soft cloth or piece of tissue paper to make sure it adheres firmly to the surface and that no paint can seep underneath.

3 Mix a pale blue wash from ultramarine blue with a hint of cadmium yellow. Using a medium flat brush, dampen the board above the masking film with clean water and then brush in vertical strokes of the pale blue mixture. While the first wash is still damp, brush more vertical blue strokes along the top of the paint and allow the paint to drift down, forming a kind of gradated wash. Leave to dry.

4 Carefully peel back the masking film from the bottom half of the painting, revealing the otter and rocks. Using a medium round brush, dampen the rocks with clean water and dot on the pale blue mixture used in Step 3.

▶

5 While the paint is still damp, use a fine round brush to dot in a darker mix of ultramarine blue and start building up tone on the rocks. Because you are working wet into wet, the colours will start to blur. Stipple a very pale cadmium yellow onto the rocks in places and leave to dry.

6 Mix a pale wash of burnt sienna and brush it over the otter's head and body. Brush over the chest area with the pale blue wash used in step 3. Leave to dry. Mix a darker brown wash from Vandyke brown and Payne's grey, and brush from shoulder to abdomen. Add a line around the back legs.

Assessment time
The base colours have now been established across the whole scene. Using the same colour (here, ultramarine blue) on both the background and the main subject creates a colour harmony that provides a visual link between the background and the foreground. You can now start to put in detail and build up the fur. In the later stages of this painting, you will want lots of crisp detail, so it's important to let each stage dry completely before you move on to the next – otherwise the paint will blur and spread.

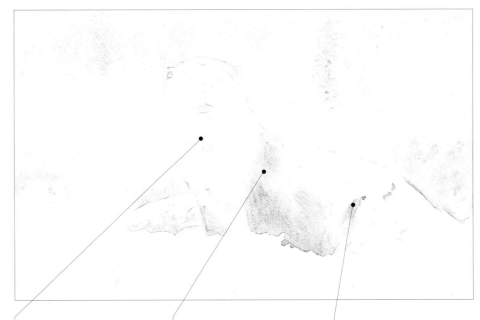

The chest, which is in shadow, is painted in a cool, pale mixture of ultramarine blue.

This darker brown helps to show the direction in which the fur is growing.

This dark line around the otter's back legs starts to establish the rounded form of the body.

7 Mix a very dark brown from Vandyke brown and Payne's grey and, using a very fine round brush, put in the dark detail on the head – the inside of the ears, the eyes and the nose. Using the same colour, start to put in short brush marks that indicate the different directions in which the fur grows.

8 Mix a warm grey from Payne's grey and a little Vandyke brown. Using a fine round brush with the bristles splayed out in a fan shape, drybrush this mixture on to the otter's chest, taking care to follow the direction of the fur.

9 Continue building up tones and textures on the otter's chest and body. Paint the lightest areas on the otter's face with permanent white gouache. Mix a light, warm brown from burnt sienna and Vandyke brown and build up tones and textures on the otter's body. Darken the facial features.

10 Mix a bright but pale blue from ultramarine blue with a hint of cadmium yellow and, using a fine round brush, brush thin horizontal lines on to the rocks on the left-hand side of the painting. This blue shadow colour helps to establish some of the crevices and the uneven surface of the rocks.

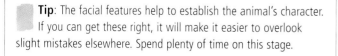

Tip: The facial features help to establish the animal's character. If you can get these right, it will make it easier to overlook slight mistakes elsewhere. Spend plenty of time on this stage.

▶

11 Mix a dark, bluish grey from Payne's grey and Vandyke brown and, using a medium round brush, paint the strands of seaweed on the rocks on the right of painting with loose, broad brushstrokes of this mixture. Leave to dry.

12 Brush a little ultramarine blue into the bottom left corner. Mix a warm brown from cadmium yellow and cadmium red and brush this mixture on to the rocks. Leave to dry. Paint lines of sea foam in permanent white gouache.

13 Now add more texture to the rock on the right, behind the otter, by stippling on a dark mixture of ultramarine blue. Note that the top of the rock, which is hit by the sunlight, is very light while the base is much darker. Using the drybrush technique, continue to add tone and form to the body of the otter, using a warm mixture of burnt sienna and ultramarine blue. Build up tone and texture on the otter's chest in the same way, using a mid-toned mixture of ultramarine blue.

14 Using a fine round brush and very short brushstrokes, paint white gouache to form the highlights along the top of the otter's back and on the body, where water is glistening on the fur. Use white gouache to paint the otter's whiskers on either side of the muzzle.

Otter

This is a fresh and lively painting that captures the animal's pose and character beautifully. The background colours of blues and greys are echoed in the shadow areas on the otter's fur, creating a colour harmony that gives the picture unity.

By including a lot of crisp detail on the otter itself and allowing the background colours of the sky and rocks to blur and merge on the paper, the artist has made the main subject stand out in sharp relief.

The background is painted in translucent, wet-into-wet washes that blur into indistinct shapes.

White gouache is used for very fine details such as the whiskers, which it would be very difficult to achieve simply by leaving the paper white.

The crisp fur detail on the otter is made up of several layers of tiny brushstrokes, worked wet on dry – a painstaking technique but one that is well worth the effort.

Flamingo

This project offers you the opportunity to practise building up layers of colour and to use your brush in a very controlled way. You need to assess the tones quite carefully when you are painting a subject that is mostly just one colour. You may find that it helps to half close your eyes, as this makes it easier to work out where the lightest and darkest areas are.

It is often a good idea to keep the background soft and blurred by using wet-into-wet washes when you are painting a textured subject like this, as the details stand out more clearly and the subject is separated from its surroundings.

Materials
- *HB pencil*
- *Hot-pressed watercolour board or smooth paper*
- *Watercolour paints: viridian, Payne's grey, cadmium red, ultramarine blue, ivory black, cadmium yellow*
- *Gouache paints: permanent white*
- *Brushes: large round, medium round, fine round, small flat, very fine*
- *Masking film (frisket paper)*
- *Scalpel or craft (utility) knife*

Preliminary sketches
Try out several compositions to decide which one works best before you make your initial underdrawing.

Reference photograph
This shot was taken in a nature reserve as reference for the feather colours. Wildlife parks and nature reserves are good places to take photos of animals and birds that you might not be able to get close to in the wild.

1 Using an HB pencil, trace your reference sketch on to hot-pressed watercolour board or smooth paper. Place masking film (frisket paper) over the whole picture area. Using a sharp scalpel or craft (utility) knife, carefully cut around the outline of the flamingo and the oval shape formed by the curve of the bird's neck. Peel back the masking film from the background, leaving the flamingo covered.

2 Take a piece of tissue paper and gently rub it over the film to make sure it is stuck down firmly and smoothly. It is essential that the background wash can't slip under the mask and on to the flamingo's body.

3 Mix a pale, watery wash of viridian. Using a large round brush, brush it over the background in long diagonal strokes, stopping about halfway down the paper.

4 Mix a pale wash of Payne's grey. While the first wash is still damp, working from the bottom of the painting upwards, brush the Payne's grey over the background, stopping at the point where it overlaps the viridian a little.

▶

5 Using a medium round brush and holding the brush almost vertically, brush long strokes of Payne's grey over the damp wash to imply the foreground grasses. The paint will blur slightly, creating the effect of an out-of-focus background. Leave to dry.

6 Remove the masking film from the flamingo. Mix a pale, watery wash of cadmium red. Using a medium round brush with a fine point, carefully brush the mixture over the flamingo's head and neck, leaving the bill and a small highlight area on the top of the head unpainted. Make sure none of the paint spills over on to the background.

7 Strengthen the colour on the bird's head and neck by applying a second layer of cadmium red. Paint the pale pink wash on to the central part of the face.

8 Using the first wash of pale cadmium red, move on to the body, making broad strokes that follow the direction of the wing feathers. Leave the highlight areas unpainted. Add a wash of Payne's grey to the bill. Leave to dry.

Assessment time
The overall base colours of the painting have been established and we are beginning to see a contrast between the blurred, wet-into-wet background and the sharper, wet-on-dry brushstrokes used on the bird, which will be reinforced as the painting progresses. Much of the rest of the painting will be devoted to building up tones and feather texture on the flamingo.

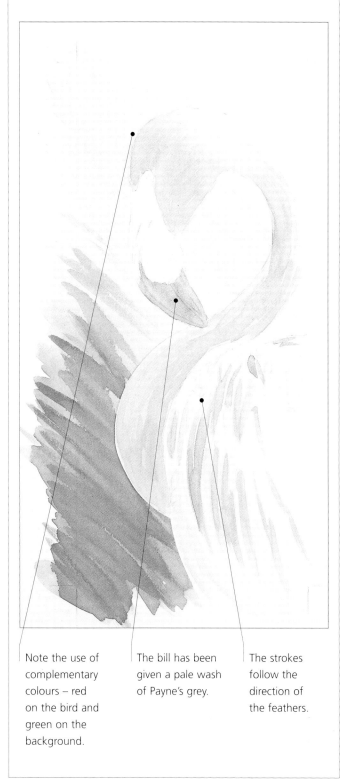

Note the use of complementary colours – red on the bird and green on the background.

The bill has been given a pale wash of Payne's grey.

The strokes follow the direction of the feathers.

9 Mix a stronger wash of cadmium red and, using a very small, almost dry, round brush, start building up the colour on the head, making tiny, evenly spaced brushstrokes to create the feeling of individual feathers. Using a small flat brush with the bristles splayed out, start working down the neck, again making tiny brushstrokes.

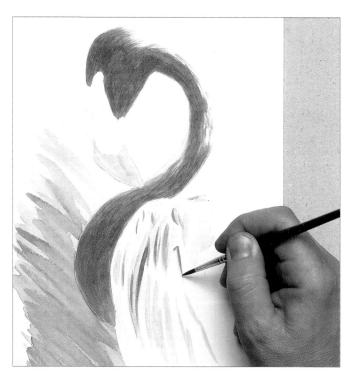

10 Continue painting the flamingo's neck, making sure that your strokes follow the direction in which the feathers grow. Using a fine round brush, paint over the main wing feathers again. Leave to dry.

▶

11 Mix a very pale pink from pale cadmium red with a little permanent white gouache and, using a fine round brush, carefully paint the area around the eye. Mix a mid-toned wash of Payne's grey and, using a fine round brush, paint the detailing on the bird's bill. Leave to dry.

12 Continue building up detail on the bill. Add a little ultramarine blue to the Payne's grey mixture and paint the shadow cast by the beak and the shadowed area on the outer edge of the bird's body. Leave to dry.

13 Mix a wash of ivory black and paint the bill, leaving spaces between your brushstrokes in order to give some texture and show how light reflects off the shiny bill. Add a dot of pale cadmium yellow for the eye.

14 Mix cadmium red with a little cadmium yellow and, using a very fine round brush, dot this mixture on to the bird's neck, just beyond the point where the initial cadmium red washes end, so that there isn't such a sharp transition from red to white. Use a fine round brush to add detail in ivory black to the eye.

15 The body looks very pale compared to the head and neck so, using a fine round brush and cadmium red, continue to build up tone on the body with tiny brushstrokes that follow the direction of the feathers. Touch permanent white gouache into the white spaces on the bird's body, leaving white paper on the right-hand side so that the image appears to fade out on the lightest side.

Flamingo

This is a beautiful example of the effectiveness of building up layers of the same colour to achieve the desired density of tone. The lovely soft texture is achieved through countless tiny brushstrokes that follow the direction of the feathers.

The composition is very effective, too. The tall, thin shape of the painting echoes the shape of the flamingo, and the viewer's eye is led in a sweeping curve from the bottom right-hand corner to the focal point – the bird's head.

Softly feathered brushstrokes soften the transition from red to white.

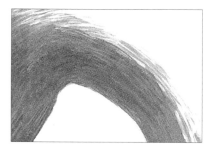

Paying careful attention to where the highlights fall has helped to make the bill look three-dimensional.

Note how gouache gives you much more control over the exact placement and size of highlights than simply leaving the paper unpainted, as you can paint over underlying colour with a very fine brush.

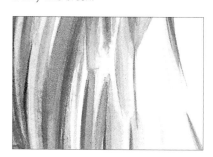

Painting Buildings

We spend our lives living and working inside buildings, but often pay them scant regard for, as long as they serve the purpose for which they were constructed, our attentions are focused elsewhere.

Buildings not only reflect function and purpose, but also the people for whom they were built. Styles can vary greatly, depending on location and the prevailing weather conditions and climate. Often, buildings can be immediately identified as belonging to a certain place – think of the palazzos of Venice or the art deco skyscrapers of New York or Chicago. They also reflect the age in which they were built and may also often give clues to the surrounding landscape and geology, as many buildings are constructed using materials that are obtained locally.

Building materials vary enormously in colour and texture. Honey-coloured dressed stone, red brick, grey concrete, flint, weathered and painted wood, steel and glass, terracotta tiles, blue-grey slate, mud and straw: the wide range makes demands on any artist and will require the use of several different techniques to successfully represent them.

Inevitably, when you are drawing and painting buildings, you will need to use both aerial and linear perspective. The idea of having to use perspective alarms some people, but once you have mastered the basic principles, the rest is relatively straightforward. Simplicity is the key, and even highly complex buildings consist, when all the intricate architectural and decorative detail has been stripped away, of a few simple geometric shapes. Try to analyse your subject in these terms before you set pencil to paper.

Draw your building in the same way and sequence in which it was constructed. First, the basic structure, then the doors and windows. Only in the very final stages should you attempt to add any decorative embellishment.

Although you do not need to become an architectural authority, it does help if you have some knowledge, no matter how rudimentary, of how buildings are constructed. It is all too easy to draw or paint a building that does not appear solid and looks as if it will fall over at any minute. This is a common mistake, particularly for novice painters.

Broadway, New York ▼
This complex painting used both aerial and linear perspective. Linear perspective creates a sense of depth, leading the eye along the avenue and into the distance. Aerial perspective enhances the effect of distance, as the colour and the detail become less pronounced the further away they are.

Grand Canal, Venice ▲
This painting of canalside buildings
in Venice was made using wet-on-dry
washes after a careful and detailed
preliminary drawing.

Tips: • Unless you are particularly
confident, begin by making a light
underdrawing to work out any problems
regarding perspective and proportion.
• Use both linear and aerial perspective.
Both will help to create an illusion of
depth, and the correct use of linear
perspective will ensure that your building
does not look as if it is about to fall over.
• Pay attention to shadows: they
contribute to the composition and will
help to establish a sense of depth.
• Use a range of watercolour techniques
to capture the texture and character of
the building and the materials used in
its construction.

Le Garde Freinet ▲
This painting of a house in a small French village uses wet-on-dry and wet-into-wet
techniques, along with careful spattering and drybrush work, to show the crumbling
plaster and weathered paint on the pale blue shutters.

Hillside town in line and wash

Line and wash is the perfect technique for this brightly coloured lakeside town, where you need fine detailing in the buildings and soft wet-into-wet washes in the surrounding landscape.

This project uses both waterproof and soluble inks, as they bring very different qualities to the image. Waterproof ink must be used in areas where you want the pen lines to remain permanent, such as the skyline and the wrought-iron balconies. Soluble ink, on the other hand, blurs and runs in unpredictable and exciting ways when you brush water or watercolour paint over it. Before you embark on any pen work, therefore, you need to think carefully about what kind of ink to use where.

In this scene, the tree-covered background is darker than the foreground. (Often in landscape paintings, you find that things in the background appear paler because of the effect of aerial perspective.) This helps to hold the image together, as it provides a natural frame around the focal point – the colourful buildings and their reflections.

Materials
- *HB pencil*
- *120lb (220gsm) good-quality drawing paper*
- *Art pen loaded with waterproof sepia ink*
- *Art pen loaded with water-soluble sepia ink*
- *Watercolour paints: ultramarine blue, cobalt blue, sap green, yellow ochre, phthalocyanine green, cadmium orange, cadmium red, burnt sienna, cadmium yellow, alizarin crimson, deep violet*
- *Brushes: medium round*

> **Tip**: If you are working from a reference photograph in which the light is very flat and bland, imagine how the light would fall on the scene on a bright sunny day. Where and how long would the shadows be? Make sure you keep your imaginary lighting consistent over the whole scene.

The original scene
This photograph was taken on a very overcast day, simply as a reference shot for the architectural details. As a consequence of the weather, the colours are dull and the light is flat and uninteresting. In situations like this, feel free to improve on what you saw at the time by making the colours brighter in your painting.

The composition pulls your eye to the edge of the picture, out into the centre of the lake.

The boat is a very stark white and detracts from the bright colours of the buildings.

The light is very flat: more contrast is needed to make the buildings look three-dimensional.

Preliminary sketch
Here the artist decided to crop in to make the composition tighter than it was in the original photograph. He also moved the boat further into the picture.

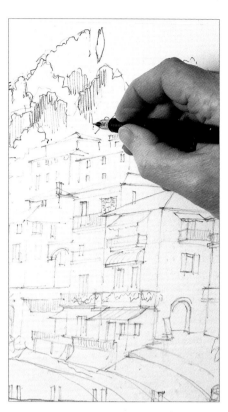

1 Using an HB pencil lightly sketch your subject, taking plenty of time to measure the relative heights and angles of the buildings carefully and making sure that you keep all the many vertical lines truly vertical. You can work much more loosely for the background hillside and trees, which will form a much softer, impressionistic backdrop to the scene.

2 Using waterproof sepia ink, put in the skyline. Using water-soluble sepia ink, put in the roofs and background trees, loosely hatching the trees to indicate the tones.

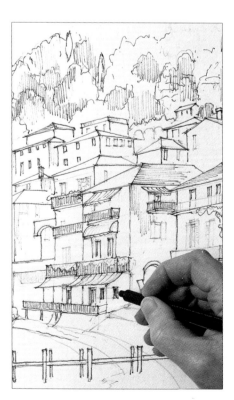

3 Continue with the line work, hatching the darkest areas of the trees in water-soluble ink, which you want to blend with paint in the later stages, and drawing the railings on the balconies in waterproof ink, so that the lines are permanent.

4 Using waterproof sepia ink, block in the windows on the shaded sides of the buildings.

▶

Assessment time
The pen work is now complete and will underpin the whole of the painting. If you have planned it properly, the lines drawn in waterproof sepia ink will be permanent, while those drawn in water-soluble ink will blur and run when washed over with watercolour paint. You cannot predict exactly how the lines will run, but this unpredictability is part of the fun and will impart great liveliness and spontaneity to the finished work.

Hatching in water-soluble ink indicates the areas of light and dark on the trees.

Waterproof ink is used for all the lines that need to be retained in the final painting.

Loose scribbles indicate the ripples in the water.

5 Mix a bright blue from ultramarine blue and cobalt blue watercolour paints. Using a medium round brush, wash this mixture over the sky, leaving some gaps for clouds. Mix a pale wash of sap green and brush it over the trees. Note how the soluble sepia ink blurs, giving the impression of the tree branches. Add a little yellow ochre to the mixture for the trees on the right-hand edge of the painting. Leave to dry.

6 Mix a dark green from ultramarine blue and phthalocyanine green and paint the tall cypress trees that stand along the skyline. The vertical lines of the trees break up the horizon and add interest to the scene. Use the same dark green mixture to loosely brush in some dark foliage tones on the trees, taking care not to allow any of the paint to spill over on to the buildings below.

7 Mix a terracotta colour from cadmium orange, cadmium red and burnt sienna. Using the tip of the brush, paint the roofs, adding more burnt sienna for the shaded sides of the roofs. Note how the whole picture begins to take on more form and depth as soon as you put in some shading.

8 Use a slightly paler version of the mixture used for the roofs to paint the shaded sides of some of the buildings. Work carefully so that you retain the sharp vertical lines of the buildings. This is an important aspect of making the buildings look three-dimensional.

9 Mix a very pale wash of yellow ochre and brush it on to the front of some of the houses. Paint the shaded sides of the terracotta-coloured houses in a mixture of yellow ochre and burnt sienna.

10 Finish painting the façades of the buildings. Mix a light green from sap green and cadmium yellow and dot in the foliage on the balconies. While this is still damp, dot on dark phthalocyanine green to build up some tone and depth.

▶

11 Paint the striped awnings in dilute washes of alizarin crimson and cobalt blue (but don't try to make the stripes on the awnings too precise and even, or the work will start to look stilted). Paint the window shutters in cobalt blue and phthalocyanine green.

12 Mix a pale but warm purple from ultramarine blue, deep violet and burnt sienna and paint the shadowed sides of the buildings and a narrow strip under the awnings. This reinforces the three-dimensional effect and separates the houses from each other and from the background.

13 Using the same colour, continue putting in the shadows on the houses and on the shoreline promenade and jetty. Paint the reflections in the water, using watered-down versions of the colours used on the buildings. Leave to dry.

14 Mix a deep blue from ultramarine blue, cobalt blue and a little deep violet. Carefully brush this over the water area, working around the boat and the posts of the jetty and leaving some gaps for broken ripples and highlights.

Hillside town in line and wash

With the addition of a few final details (the jetty, painted in a mixture of burnt sienna and ultramarine blue; the upturned boats in very pale washes of alizarin crimson and ultramarine blue, and the boat on the lake in alizarin crimson), the painting is complete. Precise pen work in both water-soluble and waterproof ink has combined with loose brushstrokes and wet-into-wet washes to create a lively rendering of this charming lakeside town.

The blurred, wet-into-wet trees focus attention on the sharply defined buildings.

Loose strokes of colour are used to depict the awnings.

Precise pen lines set down in the very earliest stages remain in the finished work.

Moroccan kasbah

The location for this striking and unusual project is the World Heritage site of Ait-Ben-Haddhou, in southern Morocco. It is a traditional-style village made up of several earthen fortresses, each one some 10 metres (30 feet) high.

With its straight-edged buildings and clean lines, the scene looks deceptively simple, but it demonstrates well how important it is to train yourself to assess tones. The earthen buildings are all very similar in colour (predominantly ochre and terracotta), so without strong contrasts of tone you will never succeed in making them look three-dimensional.

If you are painting on location, you may find that the light and, consequently, the direction and length of any shadows changes as you work. It is a good idea to make light pencil marks on your paper, just outside the margins of your painting, indicating the angle of the sun. This makes it easier to keep the lighting consistent when you are painting over a period of several hours.

Materials
- *2B pencil*
- *140lb (300gsm) NOT watercolour paper, pre-stretched*
- *Watercolour paints: cerulean blue, yellow ochre, light red, vermilion, mauve, white, alizarin crimson, Hooker's green, Winsor yellow, Payne's grey, ultramarine blue, burnt umber*
- *Brushes: large wash, medium round, medium flat, fine filbert*

Tip: Use a pencil to measure the relative heights of the buildings. Hold the pencil out in front of you and align the tip with part of your subject (say, the top of the tallest building), then run your thumb down the pencil until it aligns with the base of the building. You can transfer this measurement to your watercolour paper, again holding the pencil at arm's length. It is important to keep your arm straight and the pencil vertical, so that the pencil remains a constant distance from the subject.

The original scene
The artist took this photograph around midday, when the sun was almost directly overhead. Consequently, the colours looked somewhat bleached out and there were no strong shadows to bring the scene to life. She decided to use a little artistic licence and enhance what she saw by intensifying the colours in order to make her painting more dramatic.

The sky looks pale and doesn't have the warmth that one associates with hot African countries.

Here, the mud-brick buildings look pale and bleached out; in the right light, however, they glow a warm orangey-red.

1 Using a 2B pencil, lightly sketch the scene, taking careful note of the relative heights of the buildings and their angles in relation to one another.

2 Using a large wash brush, dampen the sky area with clean water, brushing carefully around the outlines of the buildings to get a neat, clean edge. Mix a wash of cerulean blue. After about a minute, when the water has sunk in but the paper is still damp, quickly brush on the colour. (You may want to switch to a smaller brush to paint up to the edge of the buildings. Use the side of the brush and brush the paint upwards, to avoid accidentally getting any of the blue colour on the buildings.)

3 Mix a pale but warm terracotta colour from yellow ochre, light red and a tiny amount of vermilion. Using a medium round brush, wash this mixture over the buildings, working around the fronds of the foreground palm trees and adding a little more yellow ochre as you work across from right to left.

Tip: Vary the tone of the buildings. If they are too uniform in tone they will look newly built and mass produced.

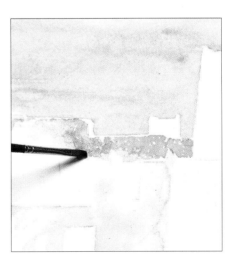

4 Add a little mauve to the mixture to make a deeper tone. Paint the wall at the base of the picture, painting around the trunks of the palm trees. Hold the brush at an angle as you do this and make jagged marks, as this helps to convey the texture of the trunks and shows that they are not straight-edged.

5 Continue working across the painting until you have put in all of the lightest tones of the buildings.

6 Mix a mid tone from yellow ochre and a tiny amount of mauve and, using a medium flat brush, stipple this mixture on to the buildings in the centre of the painting to give them some texture as well as tone. Add more mauve to the mixture for the darker left-hand side.

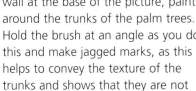

7 Brush white watercolour over the top edge of the building in the centre. This reduces the intensity of the yellow and makes it look as if it has been bleached by the sun.

8 Mix a dark terracotta from light red, yellow ochre and a touch of alizarin crimson and start painting the darkest tones – the sides of the buildings that are in deepest shade.

Assessment time

The light, mid- and dark tones are now in place across the picture and, although the tones have not yet reached their final density, we are beginning to get a clear sense of which facets of the buildings are in bright sunlight and which are in shade. From this stage onwards, you need to continually assess the tonal values as you work, because even slight changes in one area will affect the balance of the painting as a whole. Take regular breaks, propping your painting up against a wall and looking at it from a distance to see how it is developing.

Stronger contrasts of tone are needed in order for the buildings to look truly three-dimensional.

Details such as the recessed windows and doors will help to bring the painting to life.

9 Mix a very dark terracotta colour from light red, yellow ochre and a touch of alizarin crimson, and begin putting in some of the fine details, such as the door in the exterior wall and some of the small windows. You are now beginning to establish a feeling of light and shade in the painting.

10 The right-hand buildings, which are in the deepest area of shade, look too light. Darken them as necessary by overlaying more washes of the colours used previously. Also darken the mid-toned wall in the centre of the picture and put some dark windows on the light side.

11 The lightest walls now look too light in relation to the rest of the painting, so darken them with another wash of the pale terracotta mixture used in Step 3. Build up the tone gradually. You can apply more washes if necessary, but if you make things too dark there is no going back.

12 Mix a yellowy green from Hooker's green and a little yellow ochre and, using a fine filbert brush, start putting in the green palm fronds in the foreground. Make short upward flicks with the brush, following the direction in which the palm fronds grow.

▶

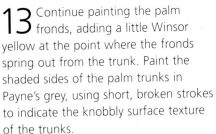

13 Continue painting the palm fronds, adding a little Winsor yellow at the point where the fronds spring out from the trunk. Paint the shaded sides of the palm trunks in Payne's grey, using short, broken strokes to indicate the knobbly surface texture of the trunks.

14 Lighten the grey by adding a little yellow ochre. Using the side of the brush, dab this mixture on to the left-hand side of the painting to indicate the scrubby texture of the bushes that grow in this area. Mix a very pale green from Payne's grey, yellow ochre and Hooker's green and dot in the side of the palm trunks that catches the light. Mix a grey-green from Payne's grey and Hooker's green and dot this mixture into the foreground shrubs. Mix a pale purple from alizarin crimson and ultramarine blue and paint the dry earth and the shadows around the base of the palm trees.

15 Mix a pale wash of alizarin crimson and darken the wall in the foreground. Feel free to use some artistic licence in your choice of colours. Although the wall is, in reality, more terracotta than pink, you are trying to put colour into a subject that doesn't have much in order to create some drama and variety in your image. Adjust the tones over the painting as a whole if you feel that it is necessary.

16 Mix a dark brown from light red and Payne's grey and put in the dark details, such as the windows. Drybrush a pale mixture of Hooker's green over the foreground to give it some tone. Mix a dark brown from burnt umber and Payne's grey and dab it on to the palm trunks to give them more tone and texture. Paint the shadows of the palm trees on the wall in a pale mixture of Payne's grey.

17 Mix a dilute wash of white watercolour paint and brush it over the tops of the highest buildings. Because the paint is transparent the underlying colour shows through, creating the effect of strong sunlight shining on the buildings and bleaching out the colour. Don't worry if the white looks too strong when you first apply it to the paper as it will quickly sink in and look natural.

Moroccan kasbah

The artist has managed to create a surprisingly wide range of tones in this painting, and this is one of the keys to its success, as the variety helps to convey not only the weathered textures of the mud bricks but also that all-important sense of light and shade. Rich, warm colours – far warmer than in the original reference photograph – help to evoke the feeling of being in a hot country. The foreground trees and bushes contrast well with the buildings in both colour and shape.

Transparent white watercolour paint allows some of the underlying colour to show through, and this creates the impression of sun-bleached brick.

In reality, this wall is the same colour as those behind. Painting it a warm pink brings it forward in the picture and helps to create an impression of distance.

Note the use of complementary colours – the orangey ochres and terracottas of the buildings against the rich cerulean blue of the sky.

Arched window

Many people would have passed by this little window in favour of something with more obvious appeal, such as brightly painted shutters or a courtyard filled with colourful blooms. The beautiful proportions of this old window, however, with its worn stonework and row of empty terracotta pots, struck an instant chord with the artist. It is proof, if proof were needed, that you can find a subject to paint wherever you go.

Why not try this approach for yourself? Instead of looking for the picturesque, deliberately set out to find a subject that most people would consider to be unsuitable for a painting – the contents of a builder's skip, perhaps, or battered tin cans in the street. Even graffiti on a brick wall or a rusting padlock on a rickety old wooden gate can be turned into intriguing, semi-abstract studies.

From a pictorial point of view, one of the most fascinating things about old, worn subjects like this is that they have wonderfully subtle colours and textures, which makes them ideal candidates for the whole spectrum of watercolour textural techniques. Spattering, sponging, stippling and a whole range of additives can all be incorporated to good effect.

This project starts by using oil pastels as resists, revealing both the texture of the paper and underlying colours. Remember to press quite hard on the oil pastels, otherwise there won't be enough oil on the paper to resist the watercolour paint applied in subsequent stages.

Materials
- *2B pencil*
- *140lb (300gsm) NOT watercolour paper, pre-stretched*
- *Soft oil pastels: light green, dark green, pale yellow, terracotta, bright orange, pink, light grey, mid-toned grey, olive green*
- *Watercolour paints: cerulean blue, dioxazine violet, Payne's grey, olive green, burnt sienna, cadmium orange, leaf green, phthalocyanine blue, cobalt blue*
- *Brushes: medium round, fine round*
- *Ruling drawing pen*
- *Masking fluid*

Preliminary sketch
This scene contains relatively few colours and lots of dense shadows. The only way to make it look realistic is to work out in advance where the darkest and lightest tones are going to be, as the artist has done in this quick tonal sketch.

1 Using a 2B pencil, lightly sketch the outline of the window with its row of terracotta flowerpots, the main blocks of stone that surround it, and the mass of plants growing on the left-hand side.

2 Dip a ruling drawing pen in masking fluid and mask the glazing bars on the window frame, the highlights on the rims of the terracotta flowerpots and the little yellow flowers on the bush on the left. Note the differing types of marks: thin straight lines for the highlights and short dots and dashes for the individual flower petals. Leave to dry.

3 Now start to put in colour and texture with soft oil pastels, pressing quite hard to ensure that enough oil is deposited on the paper to act as a resist when the watercolour paint is applied. Roughly dash in the leaf shapes, using light green for the tallest bush and a darker green for the one in the foreground. Drag pale yellow streaks across the stonework under the window. Put in some terracotta pastel on some of the bricks and the flowerpots. Draw the orange and pink flowers on the bush. Put in some light- and mid-toned grey on the worn stonework under the window.

Assessment time
With the addition of a few more pastel marks – more green on the leaves, orange on the terracotta pots, and a dark olive green in the spaces between the pots – the oil pastel stage is now complete. Oil resists water, so these colours will show through any subsequent watercolour washes. Because you are using a rough paper, some of the oil pastel lines will be broken and the texture of the paper will also be visible. Take time to check that you have included all the areas where you want texture.

Short dots and dashes convey the shapes of the leaves and flowers.

Long, broken strokes are used for the worn stonework.

4 Now for the watercolour stages. Dampen the stonework with clean water. Mix a very pale greyish blue from cerulean blue and a little dioxazine violet watercolour paints and brush this mixture over the stonework, adding a little Payne's grey for the shadowed areas and a little more violet for the foreground. Brush very pale olive green over the shadowed stonework beneath the window ledge. Applied wet into wet, the colour blurs and looks like soft lichen.

5 Mix a very pale wash of cerulean blue and paint the white woodwork of the right-hand window frame. (Leaving the frame as white paper would look too stark in relation to the rest of the image.) Mix a warm brown from burnt sienna and dioxazine violet and carefully paint the window panes, leaving some gaps for highlights reflected in the glass.

6 Mix an orangey brown from cadmium orange and dioxazine violet and paint the first terracotta flowerpot. Add Payne's grey to the mixture for the second pot in the row, which is in shadow, and burnt sienna for the third and fourth pots.

7 Note how the oil pastel marks that you applied in the early stages resist the watercolour paint, creating very realistic-looking but subtle texture in the stonework under the window and the flowerpots. The texture of the paper plays a part in this, too.

8 Mix a pale but warm grey from cerulean blue and a little dioxazine violet and wash this mixture over the stonework under the window. While the wash is still damp, brush burnt sienna over the terracotta pastel of the bricks. Allow the paper to dry slightly, add dioxazine violet to the burnt sienna wash and paint the cracks in the stonework.

9 Mix dioxazine violet with a little olive green and spatter this mixture lightly over the foreground to create some texture on the path and wall. These spatters of dark colour look like clumps of moss or small pebbles – both of which are in keeping with the somewhat derelict and dilapidated nature of the subject.

10 Mix a fairly strong wash of leaf green (which is a bright, yellowy green) and brush it over the lightest areas on the tops of the bushes. Add cerulean blue to the mixture and use this colour to paint the mid-toned leaves, taking care not to obliterate all of the light green.

11 Mix a dark green from olive green and phthalocyanine blue and dot in the darkest tones of the leaves on the background bush, making sure your brushstrokes follow the direction in which the leaves grow. You are now beginning to establish the form of the bushes.

▶

12 Add cobalt blue to the dark green used in Step 11. Paint the spaces between the leaves of the foreground bush.

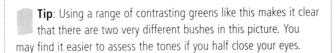
Tip: Using a range of contrasting greens like this makes it clear that there are two very different bushes in this picture. You may find it easier to assess the tones if you half close your eyes.

13 Mix a very pale wash of cerulean blue and brush it over the white spaces to the left of the bushes, which look very stark in relation to the rest of the image. Mix a very dark green from burnt sienna, olive green and a little phthalocyanine blue. Stroke this mixture on to the very darkest leaves on the foreground bush, taking the colour across the front of the window to imply overhanging leaves and branches. Leave to dry.

14 Gently rub off the masking fluid. Mix a dark purple from cobalt blue, violet and a little burnt sienna and darken some of the shadows around the window.

15 Mix a very pale wash of cerulean blue and tone down the starkness of some of the revealed whites.

Arched window

This is a beautifully controlled study in texture, painted using a relatively subdued and limited palette – proof that simplicity is often the most effective option. The empty flowerpots are what really make the picture: they provide visual interest in the foreground to hold the viewer's attention and also imply a human presence in the scene.

Using a range of greens both gives depth and indicates that there is more than one type of plant in this area.

Leaving tiny areas of window pane unpainted conveys the impression of light being reflected in the glass.

Two textural techniques, spattering and the use of resists, have been combined to good effect here.

Painting People

Portraits are often considered difficult to paint, although in reality they are no more complicated than any other subject. Part of the perceived difficulty in painting portraits comes from the need to capture a true likeness of the sitter, as somehow we expect portraits to be more lifelike, and less subject to the artist's personal interpretation, than other subjects. If you approach the subject and construct your image in the same way as any other, taking measurements and observing proportions, then that likeness should – and will – follow. Take time over your underdrawing as this is important, and observe where each facial feature is positioned in relation to the others.

A little knowledge of what the human skull is like will make it easier to position the facial features correctly. Although facial features will differ, certain measurements and proportions are approximately the same on most people.

However, a really good portrait should achieve far more than a physical likeness of the subject, it should also reveal something of the sitter's character. Hair, make-up and clothes are all important in capturing an individual's personality, and should be subject to the same scrutiny as the sitter's features.

The main watercolour techniques that you will find yourself using are wet into wet and wet on dry. Techniques that are

usually associated with making texture will, for obvious reasons, be used less often in portraiture, if at all, although drybrush can prove useful when painting hair. Watercolour is a good medium for portraits, but it requires a little forethought and planning. The traditional transparent watercolour technique of working light to dark is perfect for building up skin colours and tones, as new washes are applied over dry ones. Alternatively, flood paint colour into a wet area to create soft transitions, with one colour blending seamlessly into another. Wet-on-dry work, which creates a sharp, hard-edged focus, should be restricted to painting the features on the sitter's face.

The red shirt ▼
The boy's mischievous and adventurous character is self-evident as he hangs from a tree branch with a considerable drop beneath. Carefully placed wet-on-dry washes were used over a drawing using very light wet-into-wet watercolour paints.

> **Tips**: • Spend time plotting the facial features. If your measurements and assessment of proportion are correct, a good likeness should follow.
> • Limit yourself to one or two techniques. Use wet-into-wet washes initially, and then create sharper focus by using wet-on-dry washes as the work progresses.
> • Use gum arabic in your washes, or work on a support that has been heavily sized: this makes it easier to make corrections by washing off paint.
> • If you are painting someone in their environment, work on the background and setting at the same time as the figure per se to avoid the portrait looking as if it has simply been pasted in.

Lydia and Alice ▲

The initial work was made using wet-into-wet washes and the features were then sharpened using wet on dry. Gum arabic was used in many of the mixes. This has the effect not only of intensifying the colour but also of making the washes more transparent. Gum arabic also makes dry paint soluble if it is re-wet, so you can wash off dry paint and make any necessary corrections – this is a very useful facility when painting portraits.

Sisters ▶

Working over a careful pencil drawing using wet-on-dry washes, an overall colour harmony was achieved by using a limited range of colours. Interestingly, the two girls were painted at different times. The poses were carefully chosen so that the figures could be combined on the support.

Head-and-shoulders portrait

Painting a portrait from life for the first time can be a daunting prospect. Not only do you have the technical aspects to deal with, but you are working with a live model, who will almost certainly fidget and demand to see what you are doing. Before you embark on your first portrait session, practice drawing and painting from photographs to build up your skills and confidence.

You also have to consider your model's wellbeing. Make sure they are warm and comfortable and have adopted a pose that feels natural: they may have to hold the same pose for a long time. Ask them to fix their gaze on an object behind you (a picture on the wall, perhaps) so that, if they do move, they can easily regain their original position.

Put a lot of care into your underdrawing. If you can get the facial features in the right place and know where the main areas of light and shade are going to be, then you are well on the way to success.

Finally, don't try to do too much. Details like clothing are relatively unimportant in a head-and-shoulders portrait. Instead, try to capture your subject's mood and personality by concentrating on the eyes and expression.

Positioning the features

The sketches below are intended to provide some general guidelines to help position the facial features correctly. They are not infallible rules, however: everyone is different and you should train yourself to take objective measurements rather than relying on your preconceptions. Your viewpoint also makes a difference.

Resist the temptation to start by drawing an outline of the face. If you do this, the chances are that you will find you haven't allowed yourself enough space for the features. Start by working out the relative sizes and positions of the features and then worry about the overall outline.

It is always a good idea to put in faint pencil guidelines – a line down through the central axis of the face and lines across to mark the positions of the eyes, nose and mouth.

A large mass of hair can make things more complicated, as it is hard to work out exactly where the cranium ends and the hair begins. To begin with, try to work with a model whose hair sits close to the scalp or can be scraped back tight – or even a model with no hair at all.

Head-on view

The left and right sides of the face are not totally symmetrical, but drawing a central guideline is a good starting point.

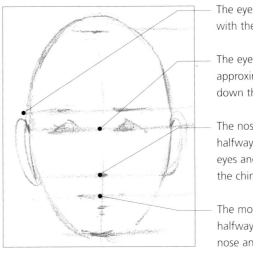

The eyes are level with the ear tips.

The eyes are approximately halfway down the facial area.

The nose is roughly halfway between the eyes and the base of the chin.

The mouth is less than halfway between the nose and chin.

Head tilted forwards

When the head is titled forward, you can see more of the cranium and less of the facial features.

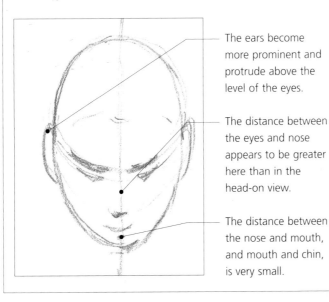

The ears become more prominent and protrude above the level of the eyes.

The distance between the eyes and nose appears to be greater here than in the head-on view.

The distance between the nose and mouth, and mouth and chin, is very small.

Head tilted backwards

When the head is tilted backwards, you can see very little of the cranium.

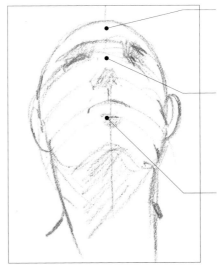

The distance between the eyes and the top of the cranium is very small from here.

The distance between the eyes and nose appears to be less here than in the head-on view.

The distance between the nose and mouth, and mouth and chin, is greater than in the head-on view.

Materials

- *HB pencil*
- *140lb (300gsm) HP watercolour paper, pre-stretched*
- *Watercolour paints: light red, yellow ochre, alizarin crimson, sap green, sepia tone, neutral tint, ultramarine blue, ultramarine violet, cobalt blue, burnt umber, cadmium orange, cadmium red*
- *Brushes: large round, medium round, fine round*

The pose

If you are new to portraiture, a simple pose, with the model looking directly at you, is probably the best way to begin. Place a strong light to one side of the model, as it will cast an obvious shadow and make it easier for you to assess areas of light and shade.

Select a plain background that does not draw attention away from your subject.

The eyes are the key to any portrait.

1 Using an HB pencil lightly sketch your subject, putting in faint construction lines as a guide to help you check that the features are accurately positioned.

2 Begin to put in some indication of the pattern in the model's blouse. You do not need to make it detailed.

> **Tip**: From time to time, look at your drawing in a mirror. This often makes it easier to assess if you have got the proportions and position of the features right. Also hold your drawing board at arm's length, with the drawing vertical, to check the perspective. When you work with the drawing board flat, the perspective sometimes becomes distorted.

3 Mix light red and yellow ochre to make the first warm but pale flesh tone. Using a medium round brush, wash this mixture over the face, neck and forearms, avoiding the eyes and leaving a few gaps for highlights. This is just the base colour for the flesh. It will look a little strange at this stage, but you will add more tones and colours later on.

▶

4 You have to work quickly at this stage to avoid the wash drying and forming hard edges. While the first wash is still damp, add more pigment and a little alizarin crimson to the first skin tone and paint the shadowed side of the face to give some modelling. Add more alizarin crimson to the mixture and paint the lips. Leave to dry.

5 Touch a little very dilute alizarin crimson on to the cheeks and some very pale sap green into the dark, shaded side of the face. Mix a warm, rich brown from sepia tone and neutral tint and start to paint the hair, leaving some highlight areas and the parting line on the top of the head completely free of paint.

6 Mix a very pale blue from ultramarine blue and a hint of ultramarine violet. See where the fabric in the blouse creases, causing shadows. Using a fine round brush, paint these creases in the pale blue mixture.

7 Go back to the hair colour mixture used in Step 5 and put a second layer of colour on the darker areas of hair. Paint the eyebrows and carefully outline the eyes in the same dark brown mixture.

8 Mix a very light green from yellow ochre with a little sap green and, using a fine round brush, paint the irises, leaving a white space for the highlight where light is reflected in the eye. Strengthen the shadows on the side of the face and neck with a pale mixture of light red and a little sap green.

9 Use the same shadow colour to paint along the edge of the nose. This helps to separate the nose from the cheeks and make it look three-dimensional. Mix ultramarine violet with sepia tone and paint the pupils of the eyes, taking care not to go over on to the whites.

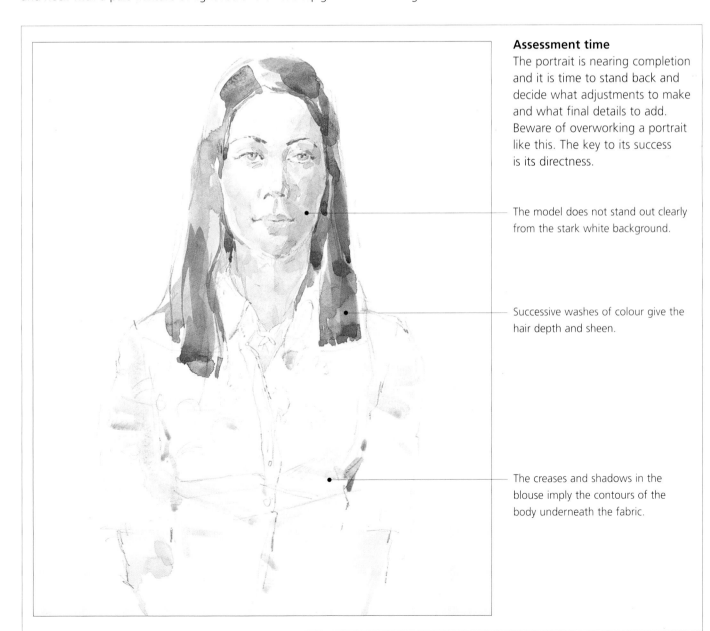

Assessment time
The portrait is nearing completion and it is time to stand back and decide what adjustments to make and what final details to add. Beware of overworking a portrait like this. The key to its success is its directness.

The model does not stand out clearly from the stark white background.

Successive washes of colour give the hair depth and sheen.

The creases and shadows in the blouse imply the contours of the body underneath the fabric.

10 Mix a dark green from sap green, cobalt blue and burnt umber. Using a large round brush, carefully wash this mixture over the background, taking care not to allow any of the paint to spill over on to the figure. (You may find it easier to switch to a smaller brush to cut in around the figure.)

11 While the background wash is still damp, add a little more pigment to the green mixture and brush in the shadow of the girl's head. Mix an orangey-red from cadmium orange and cadmium red and, using a fine round brush, start putting in some of the detail on the girl's blouse.

12 Continue building up some indication of the pattern on the girl's blouse, using the orangey red mixture from Step 11, along with ultramarine blue and sap green.

Tip: Don't try to replicate the pattern exactly: it will take far too long and will change the emphasis of the painting from the girl's face to her clothing.

Head-and-shoulders portrait

This is a sensitive, yet loosely painted portrait that captures the model's features and mood perfectly. It succeeds largely because its main focus, and the most detailed brushwork, is on the girl's eyes and pensive expression. Careful attention to the shadow areas has helped to give shape to the face and separate the model from the plain-coloured background.

The detailed painting of the eyes and mouth helps to reveal the model's mood and character.

In reality, the pattern on the blouse is much more detailed than this, but a more accurate rendition would have drawn attention away from the girl's face.

The shadow on the wall helps to separate the model from the background and gives the image more depth.

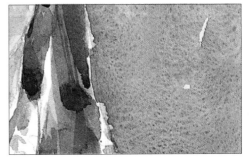

The swimmer

Although the subject of this project looks simple enough – a solitary figure swimming underwater, with relatively little discernible detail – the real interest lies in the play of light on the water and the way that shapes are slightly distorted, producing an image that tends towards abstraction. Your task is not only to capture the sleek form of the swimmer and to freeze a moment in time, but also to convey a sense of the dappled sunlight and the movement of the water.

As so often happens in painting, it helps to exaggerate certain elements in order to get across the mood that you want. Distorting the figure of the swimmer slightly in order to make it look more streamlined is one way to do this; making more of the dappled patches of sunlight on the water is another.

Adding a few drops of gum arabic to your paint mixes is a very useful technique when painting water, as it increases the gloss and transparency of watercolour paint. This, combined with the careful build-up of layers of colour, helps to make the water look as if it is shimmering in the sunlight.

Materials
- *2B pencil*
- *200lb (425gsm) NOT watercolour paper, pre-stretched*
- *Watercolour paints: cadmium lemon, alizarin crimson, cerulean blue, cobalt turquoise, cadmium red, cadmium yellow, Payne's grey, ivory black, burnt sienna, burnt umber*
- *Brushes: large round, medium round, small round*
- *Gum arabic*
- *3B graphite stick*

Reference photograph
Fascinated by the way the sunlight played on the water, the artist asked his daughter to dive repeatedly into this brightly tiled swimming pool, so that he could take reference photographs to work on at his leisure. When you are shooting a moving subject, it is hard to predict what you will actually capture on the film, so always take a lot more shots than you think you will need.

There is some dappled light on both the girl and the water, but this can be exaggerated in the painting to increase the feeling of sunlight.

Elongating the legs, arms and hands will increase the sense of movement.

Cutting off the legs at the top of the frame gives a more dynamic composition and allows the figure space into which to move.

1 Using a 2B pencil, lightly sketch the figure. Note that it is slightly distorted because of the way the light is refracted through the water. In addition, the fingers and legs have been deliberately elongated a little to create a sense of the figure moving through the water at speed.

2 Mix a light pink wash from cadmium lemon and alizarin crimson, and a slightly redder version of the same mixture. Using a medium round brush, wash these colours over the whole of the body, alternating between the two mixtures to give some tonal variety. Leave to dry.

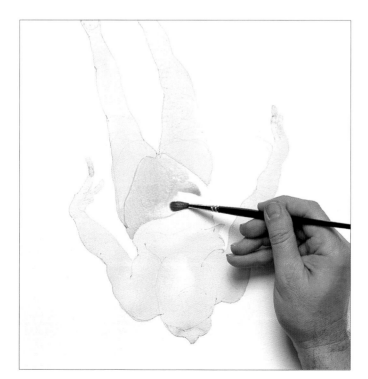

3 Mix a strong wash of cadmium lemon and add a little of the lighter pink wash used in Step 2. Using a medium round brush, paint the girl's bikini bottoms in this colour. Leave to dry.

4 Mix a large quantity of a pale blue wash from cerulean blue and a little cobalt turquoise. Wash this mixture over the whole of the background, taking care not to allow any of the paint to go over the figure. (You may need to switch to a smaller brush to "cut in" around the edges of the figure.)

▶

5 Mix three flesh tones from the following colours: alizarin crimson and cadmium lemon; alizarin crimson and a little cerulean blue; cadmium red and cadmium yellow. Dot a small amount of gum arabic into each mixture. Using a medium round brush and alternating between the three mixtures, start to paint over the girl's legs, leaving the base colour showing through in highlight areas. It doesn't matter too much which colour you use where, but try to reserve the darker mixtures for shadow areas.

6 Continue in this way until you have finished painting the legs. Leave to dry.

> **Tip**: Some of the washes may look very dark when you first apply them, but watercolour always dries to a slightly lighter tone. To be on the safe side, test your mixtures on a piece of scrap paper and leave to dry before applying them to the painting.

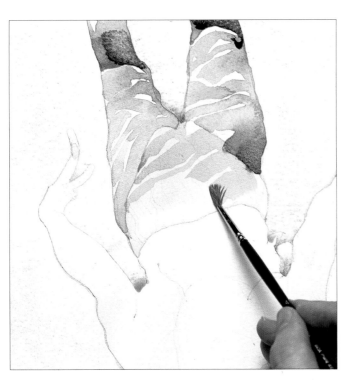

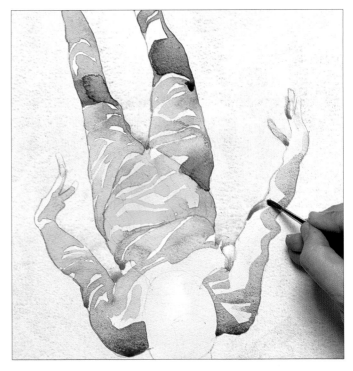

7 Mix a greenish yellow from cadmium lemon with a little Payne's grey. Using a small round brush, paint the ripples of light that run across the bikini bottoms.

8 Using a small round brush and the same flesh tones that you mixed in Step 5, paint the girl's arms and back, leaving some of the underlying wash showing through.

Assessment time

The underpainting is almost complete. The figure stands out well against the pale blue background of the water and is starting to take on a three-dimensional quality. The next stage is to redefine the form by using slightly darker mixtures and to start to put in some of the details.

Varying the flesh tones gives the figure form.

The base colour alone is visible in the most strongly lit areas.

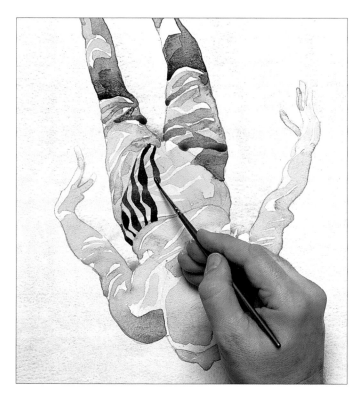

9 Mix slightly darker versions of the flesh tones used in Step 5 and work over the body again, in the same way as before. Mix a warm black from ivory black with a little Payne's grey and paint the stripes on the bikini bottoms. Note that the stripes are not straight lines. This is partly because the pattern is distorted by the way the light refracts from the water and partly because the fabric clings to the girl, helping to indicate the contours of her body.

10 Mix a rich, dark brown from burnt sienna and burnt umber and, using a medium round brush, paint the girl's hair. Leave some areas unpainted and apply a second layer of colour in others so that the hair is not a solid mass of the same tone of brown.

▶

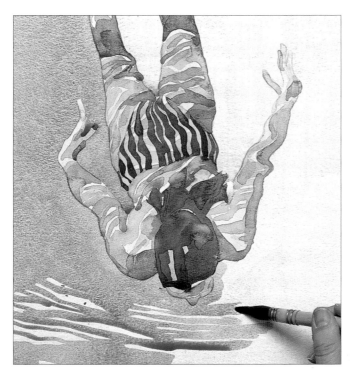

11 Mix a bright blue from cerulean blue and cobalt turquoise and, using a large round brush, begin to wash this mixture over the background. Leave some areas untouched in the top left-hand side, where sunlight dapples the water, and paint ripples in front of the girl's head to show how the water is displaced as she moves through it.

12 Continue working around the figure with the same blue mixture until you have been over the whole of the background. As in Step 4, you may find that you need to switch to a smaller brush in order to paint right up to the edge of the figure, as you must take care not to allow any of the blue mixture to spill over on to the figure. Leave to dry.

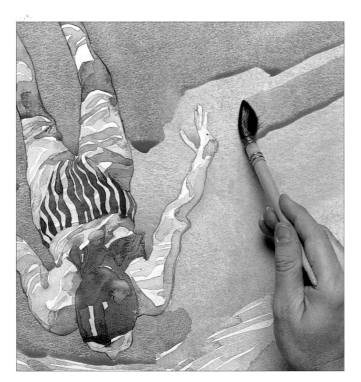

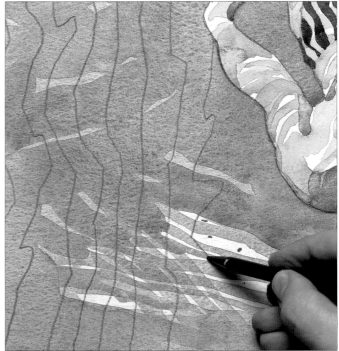

13 Mix a stronger version of the cerulean blue and cobalt turquoise mixture used in Step 11 and add a few drops of gum arabic. Paint over the background again, leaving a few spaces here and there to give the effect of dappled light. Leave to dry.

14 Using a 3B graphite stick, draw the lines of the tiles on the base of the pool. Note that, because of the way the light is refracted and the effects of perspective, the lines are not straight. The lines in the distance slope inwards because this area of the painting is further away from the viewer.

The swimmer

This is a graphic depiction of a swimmer slicing through water, the impression of speed reinforced by a deliberate distortion of her figure and the energetic ripples in front of her head. There is a wonderful feeling of light and warmth in this painting, achieved through the careful build-up of layers of colour.

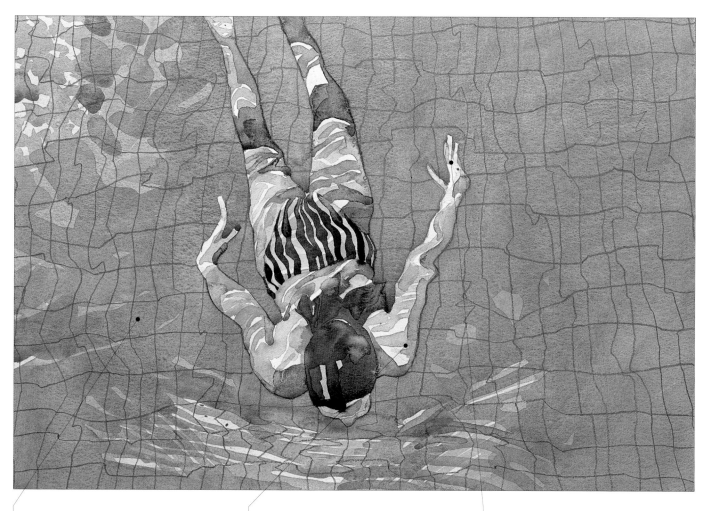

Because of the effects of perspective, the lines of the tiles slope inwards.

The effect of dappled sunlight is created by applying only one or two layers of colour to certain areas.

The swimmer's hands, arms and legs are slightly elongated, which helps to give the impression of movement.

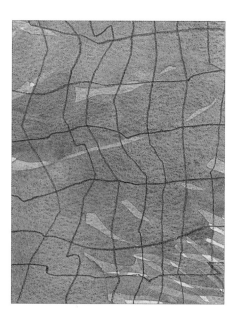

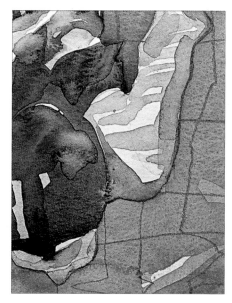

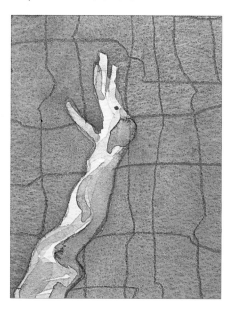

Seated figure in interior

Painting someone in a setting gives you the opportunity to say much more about them than you can in a straightforward head-and-shoulders portrait. For example, you might choose to include things that reveal something about your subject's interests – a keen musician with a guitar, perhaps, or an antiques collector surrounded by some of his or her most treasured possessions – or their work. In a domestic setting, the décor of the room itself is very often a reflection of your subject's tastes and personality.

The most important thing is not to allow the surroundings to dominate. The focus of the painting must remain on the person. This usually means that you have to deliberately subdue some of the detail around your subject, either by using muted or cool colours for the surroundings, so that your subject becomes more prominent, or, if the setting is very cluttered, by leaving some things out of your painting altogether.

Materials
- *3B pencil*
- *Rough watercolour board*
- *Watercolour paints: raw umber, alizarin crimson, cobalt blue, lemon yellow, phthalocyanine blue*
- *Brushes: medium flat, Chinese, fine round, old brush for masking*
- *Masking fluid*
- *Craft (utility) knife or scalpel*
- *Sponge*

Reference photographs
Here the artist used two photographs as reference – one for the seated, semi-silhouetted figure and one for the shaft of light that falls on the table top. Both photographs are dark and it is difficult to see much detail, but they show enough to set the general scene and give you scope to use your imagination. Instead of slavishly copying every last detail, you are free to invent certain aspects of the scene, or to embellish existing ones.

The highlight on the figure's hair is very atmospheric.

The shaft of bright sunlight illuminates part of the table top while almost everything else is in deep shade.

1 Using a 3B pencil, lightly sketch your subject, making sure you get the tilt of her head and the angles of the table, papers and books right.

2 Mix a warm, pinky orange from raw umber and alizarin crimson. Using a medium flat brush, wash it over the background, avoiding the highlight areas on the window. Add more alizarin crimson to the mixture for the warmest areas, such as the girl's shirt and the left-hand side of the curtain, and more raw umber for the cooler areas, such as the wall behind the girl and the glazing bars on the window. Leave to dry.

3 Mix a very pale green from cobalt
blue and lemon yellow and, using
a Chinese brush, paint the lightest
foliage shades outside the window,
remembering to leave some white areas
for the very bright sky beyond.

Tip: To enhance the impression of
light coming through the window,
take care not to paint foliage right up to
the edge of the window frame.

Assessment time
Mix a very pale blue from cobalt blue
and a touch of raw umber and put in
the cooler tones inside the room – the
left-hand side, which the shaft of sunlight
coming through the window doesn't
reach, and the shadows under the table.
Leave to dry.

You have now established the warm
and cool areas of the painting, which you
will build on in all the subsequent stages.
Because of her position within the frame
(roughly in the first third), the girl is the
main focus of interest in the painting,
even though she is largely in shadow.
Keep this at the forefront of your mind
as you begin to put in the detail and as
you continually assess the compositional
balance while painting.

This area is left unpainted, as it receives the
most direct sunlight.

The warm colour of the girl's shirt helps to
bring her forwards in the painting.

The shadow areas are the coolest in tone.
They recede.

4 Mix a warm brown from alizarin crimson and raw umber and paint the girl's hair. Mix a rich red from alizarin crimson, cobalt blue and a little raw umber and, using a Chinese brush, paint the curtain. Apply several vertical brushstrokes to the curtain, wet into wet, to build up the tone and give the impression that it hangs in folds.

5 Using the same red mixture, paint the shoulders and back of the girl's shirt. Add more raw umber to the mixture and paint the shadow area between the wall and the mirror, immediately behind the girl. Mix a warm blue from phthalocyanine blue and a little alizarin crimson, and paint the dark area beneath the table using loose brushstrokes.

6 Using an old brush, "draw" the shapes of leaves in the bottom left-hand corner in masking fluid. Leave to dry. Mix a rich, dark brown from raw umber and a little alizarin crimson and, using a fine round brush, paint the darkest areas of the girl's hair.

7 Add a little raw umber to the mixture for the lighter areas of hair around the face. Build up the shadow areas in the foreground of the scene, overlaying colours as before. Darken the girl's shirt in selected areas with the alizarin crimson, cobalt blue and raw umber mixture.

8 Mix a mid-toned green from phthalocyanine blue and lemon yellow and, using a fine round brush, dot this mixture into the foliage that can be seen through the right-hand side of the window. Mix a very pale purplish blue from pthalocyanine blue and a little alizarin crimson and darken the glazing bars of the window.

9 Paint the area under the window in a warm mixture of alizarin crimson and phthalocyanine blue. Mix a dark, olive green from raw umber and phthalocyanine blue and, making loose calligraphic strokes, paint the fronds of the foreground plant. Brush a very dilute version of the same mixture on to the lower part of the mirror. Build up the background tones.

10 Mix a muted green from phthalocyanine blue and lemon yellow. Brush it over the background behind the girl. Because the green is relatively cool, it helps to separate the girl from the background. It also provides a visual link between this area and the foliage on the right.

11 Paint a few vertical strokes on the curtain in a dark mixture of alizarin crimson and phthalocyanine blue. This helps to make the highlight on top of the pile of books stand out more clearly. Mix a warm brown from raw umber and phthalocyanine blue and paint under the window.

12 Rub off the masking fluid from the bottom left-hand corner. Continue building up the tones overall, using the same paint mixtures as before and loose, random brushstrokes to maintain a feeling of spontaneity.

▶

13 Mix a very pale wash of raw umber and lightly brush it on to some of the exposed areas in the bottom left-hand corner. Build up more dark tones in the foreground, using the same mixtures as before.

14 Using a craft (utility) knife or scalpel, carefully scratch off some of the highlights on the bottle on the table. Paint the wall behind the girl in a pale, olivey green mixture of raw umber and phthalocyanine blue.

15 Brush a little very pale cobalt blue into the sky area so that this area does not look too stark and draw attention away from the main subject.

16 Continue building up tones by overlaying colours. Use very loose brushstrokes and change direction continually, as this helps to convey a feeling of the dappled light that comes through the window.

17 Using a 3B pencil, define the edges of the papers on the table. Mix a very pale wash of phthalocyanine blue and, using a fine round brush, carefully brush in shadows under the papers on the table to give them more definition. Dip a sponge in a blue-biased mixture of phthalocyanine blue and alizarin crimson and gently press it around the highlight area on the floor to suggest the texture of the carpet.

Seated figure in interior
There is a wonderful sense of light and shade in this painting, and the loose brushstrokes give a feeling of great freshness and spontaneity. The scene is beautifully balanced, both in terms of its distribution of colours and in the way that dark and light areas are counterposed.

Sunlight pours through the window, illuminating the books and papers. Much of this area is left unpainted.

Pale, cool colours on the wall help to differentiate the girl from the background.

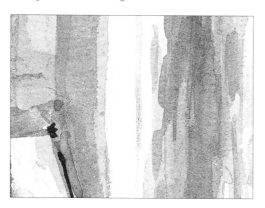

The foreground is loosely painted with overlayed colours, creating a feeling of spontaneity.

Indian market scene

Full of hustle and bustle, often packed with colourful displays of fruit, vegetables and other goods, street markets are a wonderful source of inspiration for artists – but with so much going on, it is often very difficult to work in situ. And even if you do manage to find a quiet spot to set up your easel, the chances are that you will soon find yourself surrounded by a crowd of curious onlookers, which can be somewhat intimidating.

This is one situation where it is useful to take reference photos, as you can work quickly and unobtrusively, and gather a whole wealth of material to paint from at a later date. Start with distant views and gradually move in closer to your chosen subject – and don't forget about things like advertisements, hand-written signs and unusual produce, all of which can add a lot of atmospheric local detail to your paintings.

If you want to take photographs of people, it is always best to ask their permission, although this does bring with it the risk that your subjects will start playing up to the camera. If this happens, take a few "posed" shots first and then, when they have turned back to their business, take a few more. Another good tip is to set your camera on its widest setting and point it slightly to one side of the person you are photographing. You will appear to be looking somewhere else, but the camera's field of view will be wide enough to include them in the frame, too. Above all, don't stint on the number of shots you take: film is inexpensive and if you've got a digital camera, there are no processing costs at all.

Materials
- *4B pencil*
- *90lb (185gsm) rough watercolour paper, pre-stretched*
- *Watercolour paints: indigo, alizarin crimson, raw umber, cobalt turquoise, cadmium red, Hooker's green, cadmium yellow, burnt umber, cobalt blue*
- *Gouache paints: Bengal rose, permanent white*
- *Brushes: Chinese, fine round*
- *Household candle*

Reference photographs
Here the artist used two photographs. The one on the right shows the corner of the stall and the stallholder selling his wares, and the one below shows the two ladies shopping and rows of colourful bowls of powdered dyes. In her compositional sketch, the artist angled the bowls to provide a more gentle lead-in to the picture.

The stallholder is just visible. He will be more prominent in the painting.

There is nothing of interest in this area.

A more gentle lead-in will be provided if the bowls start in the bottom right corner of the image.

1 Using a 4B pencil, sketch the subject, taking care to get the perspective right. Note how the bowls of powder get smaller and closer together as they recede into the distance.

 Tip: To make it easier to get the shapes of the bowls of powder right, think of them as simple geometric shapes – ovals with rough triangular shapes on top.

2 Mix a warm, greyish blue from indigo, alizarin crimson and a little raw umber and start putting in the cool background colours. Paint the area of deepest shade under the table, adding more raw umber to the mixture for the pavement area. This neutral background will help to unify the painting. With so many vibrant colours in the scene, the overall impact could easily be overwhelming.

3 Add more alizarin crimson to the mixture to make a darker, brown colour and brush in the shadows under the bowls and the wooden vertical supports of the shelves in the background. Use a paler version of the mixture to paint the stallholder's shirt and a darker one to paint the background of the more distant stall and the area immediately behind the stallholder's head. Filling in the negative spaces in this way makes it easier to see what it is happening in such a complicated scene.

4 Mix a warm shadow colour from indigo with a tiny amount of alizarin crimson and paint the shadows under the steel bowls, taking care to leave highlights on the rims. Use the same mixture to paint lines in between the oblong dishes of powder in the background.

5 Using an ordinary household candle, stroke candle wax over the lightbulbs. Press firmly so that enough of the wax adheres to the paper. The wax will act as a resist. The white paper will show through in places, while other areas will take on the surrounding colour, as if that colour is reflected in the glass of the bulb.

▶

Assessment time

Using the same basic mixtures as before, continue putting in some background colours and the shadows under the bowls. The basis of the background is now complete, both tonally and compositionally.

Blocking in the negative spaces makes it easier to see what is happening in the rest of the scene.

We "read" this shaded area as being on a different plane to the stall top, which is in bright sunlight.

Although the bowls are empty at this stage, their shapes and shadows are clearly established.

6 Mix a warm, purplish black from alizarin crimson and indigo and paint the stallholder's hair. Mix cadmium red with alizarin crimson and paint the wooden support on the right-hand edge of the foreground stall. Drybrush a little of the same colour on to the stall top, where powder has been spilt, and start putting the same colour into the bowls of powder. Paint cobalt turquoise on the walls at the far end.

Tip: While you have one colour mix on your palette, see where else you can use it in the painting.

7 Mix a wash of Hooker's green and paint the green plastic that covers the basket on the ground and the mounds of green powder. Mix a warm orange from cadmium red and cadmium yellow and dot the mixture into the background immediately behind the stallholder to indicate the packages on sale. (A hint of the basic shape and colour is sufficient.) Add a little burnt umber to the orange mixture and paint the stallholder's face.

8 Paint the women's skin tones in the same orangey-brown mixture. Mix a strong purple from Bengal rose gouache and cobalt blue watercolour and paint the sari worn by the woman in the foreground, leaving a few highlight areas untouched.

9 Using the same mixture and a fine round brush, paint the creases in the sari, adding more cobalt blue to the mixture for the very darkest creases. By darkening the tones in this way, you will begin to imply the folds in the fabric. Mix a dark purple from Bengal rose, alizarin crimson and a little indigo and dot in the pattern on the sari. Mix Bengal rose with a tiny amount of cobalt blue and paint the mounds of very bright pink powder.

10 Continue painting the powders, mixing cadmium red with Bengal rose for the red powders and using cobalt blue for the blue ones. Don't worry too much about the shapes of the mounds at this stage. This will become clearer as you build up the tones later on.

11 Build up the tones on the powders, using the same mixtures as before. Using a 4B pencil, draw the lines of the plastic-wrapped packages on the corner of the stall. Mix a pale wash of cobalt turquoise and brush over the lines, using a fine round brush.

▶

12 Mix a dark purple colour from Bengal rose, alizarin crimson and a little indigo. Using a fine round brush, accentuate the creases in the sari fabric in the same colour.

13 Using a mixture of alizarin crimson and indigo, paint around the stallholder. Darkening the background in this way helps to make him stand out from his surroundings. Use the same alizarin crimson and indigo mixture to strengthen the shadows on the right-hand side of the stall.

14 By this stage, all you need to do is refine some of the details. Mix a rich, brownish black from alizarin crimson, indigo and cadmium red and darken the stallholder's hair. Darken his skin tones with a more dilute version of the same mixture. Paint the stripes on the colourful woven basket in Bengal rose gouache and darken the tones on the wooden posts of the stall.

15 Tone down the brightness of the paper, where necessary, with very pale washes of the background colours. Paint the highlights on the lightbulbs in permanent white gouache.

Indian market scene

Here, the artist has created a lively interpretation of a busy market, packed with colourful sights and people going about their daily business. The composition is much more satisfactory than that of the original reference photographs.

The line of bowls leads diagonally through the image to the two women, while the stallholder is positioned near enough to the intersection of the thirds to provide a secondary focus of interest for the painting.

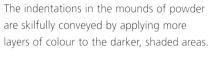

The contrast between light and dark areas establishes the different planes of the image.

The stallholder's direct gaze encourages us to follow his line of sight across the scene to the two women.

The indentations in the mounds of powder are skilfully conveyed by applying more layers of colour to the darker, shaded areas.

Glossary

Additive
A substance added to paint to alter characteristics such as the paint's drying time and viscosity. Gum arabic is a commonly used additive in watercolour painting.

Body colour
Opaque paint, such as gouache, which can obliterate underlying paint colour on the paper.

Colour
Complementary: colours that lie opposite one another on the colour wheel.
Primary: a colour that cannot be produced by mixing other colours, but can only be manufactured. Red, yellow and blue are the three primary colours.
Secondary: a colour produced by mixing equal amounts of two primary colours.
Tertiary: a colour produced by mixing equal amounts of a primary colour and the secondary colour next to it on the colour wheel.

Composition
The way in which the elements of a drawing or painting are arranged within the picture space. The composition does not need to be true to real life.

Closed composition: one in which the eye is held deliberately within the picture area.
Open composition: one that implies that the subject or scene continues beyond the confines of the picture area.

Drybrush
The technique of dragging an almost dry brush, loaded with very little paint, across the surface of the paper to make textured marks.

Format
The shape of a painting. The most usual formats are landscape (a painting that is wider than it is tall) and portrait (a painting that is taller than it is wide), but panoramic (long and thin) and square formats are also common.

Gouache see Body colour.

Ground
The prepared surface on which an artist works. See also Support.

Highlight
The point on an object where light strikes a reflective surface. In watercolour painting, highlights are often left as white paper.

Hue
A colour in its pure state, unmixed with any other.

Line and wash
The technique of combining watercolour washes with pen-and-ink work.

Mask
Any substance that is applied

to paper to prevent paint from reaching specific areas. Unlike resists, masks can be removed when no longer required. There are three materials used for masking – masking tape, masking fluid and masking film – although, depending on the techniques you are using and the effect you want to create, you can simply cover up the relevant part of the painting by placing a piece of paper over it.

Overlaying
The technique of applying layers of watercolour paint over washes that have already dried in order to build up colour to the desired strength.

Palette
(1) In watercolour painting, a ceramic or plastic container in which paint colours are mixed.
(2) The range of colours used by an artist.

Pan
A small, rectangular container in which watercolour paint is sold.

Paper
The commonly used support for watercolour paintings.
HP (hot-pressed): The smoothest type of watercolour paper. HP paper is particularly good for fine brushwork.

NOT: This shortened name stands for "not hot-pressed". It is a slightly textured paper.

Rough: The most textured type of watercolour paper.

Tinted: Although watercolour paper is normally white, tinted watercolour paper is available in a small range of pale colours.

Weight: The weight of a paper is normally given in pounds per ream (a ream being 500 sheets) or grams per square metre. The heavier the watercolour paper, the more water it can absorb. Papers under 140lb (300gsm) need to be stretched before use to prevent them buckling when water is applied.

Perspective
A system whereby artists can create the illusion of three-dimensional space on the two-dimensional surface of the paper.

Aerial perspective: the way the atmosphere, combined with distance, influences the appearance of things. This is also known as atmospheric perspective.

Linear perspective: linear perspective exploits the fact that objects appear to be smaller the further away they are from the viewer. The system is based on the fact that all parallel lines, when extended from a receding surface, meet at a point in space known as the vanishing point. When such lines are plotted accurately on the paper, the relative sizes of objects will appear correct in the painting.

Resist
A substance that prevents one medium from touching the paper beneath it. Wax (in the form of candle wax or wax crayons) is the resist most commonly used in watercolour painting; it works on the principle that wax repels water.

Sgraffito
The technique of scratching off paint to reveal either an underlying paint colour or the white of the paper. The word comes from the Italian verb *graffiare*, which means "to scratch".

Shade
A colour that has been darkened by the addition of black or a little of its complementary colour.

Spattering
The technique of flicking paint on to the paper to create texture.

Sponging
The technique of applying colour to the paper with a sponge, rather than with a brush, in order to create a textured appearance.

Stippling
The technique of applying dots of colour to the paper, using just the tip of the brush.

Support
The surface on which a painting is made (normally paper in watercolour painting).

Tint
A colour that has been lightened. In pure watercolour, a colour is lightened by by adding water to the paint.

Tone
The relative lightness or darkness of a colour.

Underdrawing
A drawing made as a guide to where to apply the paint.

Wash
A thin layer of transparent paint that usually covers a large area of the painting.

Flat wash: an evenly laid wash that exhibits no variation in tone.

Gradated wash: a wash that gradually changes in intensity from dark to light or (less commonly) vice versa.

Variegated wash: a wash that changes from one paint colour to another.

Wet into wet
The technique of applying paint on to wet paper or on top of an earlier wash that is still damp.

Wet on dry
The technique of applying paint to dry paper or on top of an earlier wash that has dried completely.

Index